Early Detection

Prevention and Amelioration of Mental Health Conditions in Young People

Ann R. Poindexter, M.D.

Early Detection

Prevention and Amelioration of Mental Health Conditions in Young People

Ann R. Poindexter, M.D.

TABLE OF CONTENTS

FOREWORD

In the past few years I have noticed an increasing numbers of articles about diagnosing psychiatric disorders in children very early. I began to think about the importance of looking at this for children with various developmental disabilities, including autism spectrum disorders, as well as children in the general population. I have gathered together in this book some of the research dealing with this, but this is not by any means all the research that is being done—every month brings more and more articles. I've tried to emphasize early diagnosis, since this is our best chance to prevent or ameliorate significant symptoms and help children have better and more productive lives. I have included virtually no discussion about medication treatment, since this is a whole other issue. Before we can treat we really do need to have a valid diagnostic postulate, and while we don't want to deny children appropriate medication when needed, we certainly don't want to just "throw medication at behavior."

The chapters are not of equal length, since some diagnoses have been far more intensively researched than have others. Information about the incidence of psychiatric disorders in adults is included in some chapters. I feel that if we realize what a major problem these conditions represent we will realize the potentially significant benefits of prevention or at least early diagnosis with subsequent efforts to ameliorate later problems.

I hope this book will be helpful for the large group of us who work with children and adolescents, both those with and without developmental disabilities. While much of it is based on review of medical literature, I hope that it will be helpful for non-medical professionals, such as psychologists, social workers, special education professionals, academics in these fields, and parents, as well as primary care physicians and psychiatrists.

—Ann Poindexter

CHAPTER 1

INTRODUCTION

The High Toll of Mental Illness

Mental illness contributes a substantial burden of disease worldwide, with about 450 million people having mental disorders at any given time. At least one fourth of the world's population will develop a mental or behavioral disorder at some point during their lives. Mental disorders account for about 25% of disability in North America and western Europe. An estimated one in ten children in the U.S. has a mental disorder that causes some level of impairment, and the effects of mental illness are evident across the life span, among all ethnic, racial, and cultural groups, as well as among people of every socioeconomic level. Mental illness costs the U.S. an estimated $150 billion dollars every year, excluding the costs of research (Centers for Disease Control and Prevention, 2005a).

Behavioral and Developmental Problems Can Effect Health,
Quality of Life, and Ability to Access Care

The needs of children with emotional, behavioral, and developmental problems are a national and international concern. These emotional, behavioral, and developmental problems can affect a child's health. In order to assess the health care and well-being of those children in the United States with problems serious enough to require treatment or counseling, researchers from Oregon Health and Science University and CDC analyzed parent-reported data from a 2001 national survey. They found that, when compared with children with other special health care needs, children with chronic emotional, behavioral, and developmental problems were more likely to have diminished health and quality of life and to have problems accessing and receiving needed care (Centers for Disease Control and Prevention, 2005b). Not surprisingly, children from families of lower socioeconomic status have disproportionately higher rates of unmet needs (Ganz & Tendulkar, 2006).

Future Psychiatric Disorders May Be Predictable

A research group in Finland studied the rate of, and factors associated with, recognition of psychiatric disorders and self-perceived problems among 2347 eighteen-year-old boys. The group was assessed at age eight by parents and teachers on Rutter scales, and self-reports using the Child Depression Inventory. At military call-up 10 years later, the boys filled in the Young Adult Self-Report, and information about recognized psychiatric disorders was obtained from the national military register. About 4.6% of boys were recognized as having a psychiatric disorder at the military call-up medical exam, and 23.1% of boys reported emotional, behavioral, or relational difficulties but not to the degree that a diagnosis could be made. All informant sources, parents, teachers, and the children themselves at age eight, independently predicted recognition of psychiatric disorders and perceived difficulties ten years later (Sourander et al., 2005).

Coordination Can Improve Access to Assessment and Treatment

Children with disabilities of any sort, particularly developmental and/or intellectual disabilities, often have a great deal of difficulty obtaining assessment for and treatment of psychiatric/behavioral disorders. In a study of community-dwelling children with disabilities, Witt, Kasper, and Riley (2003) examined the use of mental health services and correlates of receiving services. The study sample included 4,939 children with disabilities, ages 6 to 17 years, representing an estimated eight million children with disabilities nationwide. Parents of these children reported on health, emotional and behavioral problems, mental health services use, and who, if anyone, coordinated the child's health care. Among the 11.5% of disabled children with poor psychosocial adjustment, only 11.8% had received mental health services in the previous year. Younger and African-American disabled children were less likely to receive mental health services. No data are presently available for the likelihood of Hispanic children to receive services, but they probably are also not very likely to receive services. Service use was more likely if a health professional coordinated care than if there was only a family member or no one coordinating care. Services were even more apt to be used if care was jointly coordinated by a family member and a health professional. While inequalities of access to mental health services do exist, the school setting may be one in which some barriers to mental health services for disabled children are reduced.

The Complex Impact of Environmental Influences

Any difficulty with obtaining assessment and treatment is particularly troubling in view of the high cost of mental health disorders, both personally and fiscally. This is especially true since recent research indicates that mental health disorders are generally not of single-factor origin—both "nature and nurture" are involved, and early recognition may lead to far more effective treatment. Pennington (2002) points out that all *DSM-IV-TR* (American Psychiatric Association, 2000) diagnoses are described in behavioral terms and that the etiology of all behaviorally defined disorders includes both genetic and environmental influences. While the genetic influences probably cannot be controlled, environmental influences, when discovered, may be addressed to improve outcomes—either to prevent disorders or improve eventual outcomes of disorders. As an example, a group from Western Michigan University looked at children who had been exposed prenatally to alcohol, some of whom were also exposed to postnatal traumatic experience, and found that those with both pre- and postnatal experiences had lower intelligence scores and more severe neurodevelopmental deficits in language, memory, visual processing, motor skills, and attention than did traumatized children without prenatal alcohol exposure; those with pre- and postnatal experiences also exhibited more oppositional/defiant behavior, inattention, hyperactivity, impulsivity, and social problems (Henry, Sloan, & Black-Pond, 2007). Also, early recognition and treatment may be particularly beneficial, since every year of development without illness allows time for the child to develop ego skills to deal with his/her inherited risk factors (Wamboldt & Reiss, 2006).

Even for conditions that are very inheritable, the presence of the condition in identical twins is substantially lesss than 100%, which shows that nongenetic factors also contribute to the conditions (Smoller & Korf, 2008).

The Importance of Early Treatment

The term "prevention" traditionally was used for intervention applied before the onset of a clinically diagnosable disorder in order to reduce the number of new cases of the disorder. More recently, preventive methods are viewed as attempts to prevent entry to, or progression along, the pathway to a severe, debilitating psychological disorder. Currently the National Institute for Mental Health (NIMH)'s definition of prevention research has broadened beyond preventing onset to preventing relapse, disability, and co-morbidity among people already diagnosed with a mental health disorder. From both an economic and social perspective, prevention or amelioration of illness is clearly more desirable than treatment of diseases that are chronic or that have an episodic course (Boyce, Heinssen, Ferrell, & Nakamura, 2007).

Routine Assessment and Barriers to Early Intervention

Assessment methodology currently exists to routinely screen very young children in primary health care settings and early intervention programs for social-emotional and behavior problems as well as for delays in the acquisition of competencies. Unfortunately, despite the likely long-term benefits and cost-saving potential of early identification and intervention services, short-term costs and knowledge barriers currently limit widespread implementation (Carter, Briggs-Gowan, & Davis, 2004). Also, even when screening is done in the primary care setting, when the screening shows intellectual disability and/or autism, the screening process usually stops there, unfortunately, and exploration of further conditions does not continue. The National Center for Education in Maternal and Child Health of Georgetown University published a practice guide and tool kit in 2002 (Jellinek, Patel, & Froehle, a & b) which contain a wealth of information for clinicians and materials for families and others dealing with children with mental health problems which are quite applicable to children with all sorts of developmental disabilities.

While routine assessment for psychopathology is not widespread, a number of interesting pilot programs have been reported in recent years. Screening for various conditions will be discussed in later chapters in this volume.

Research About the Brains of Children

Studying the brains of children in general, the largest systematic clinical study ever performed concerning the neurobiology of young people was being finished up in the summer of 2007. In this study, researchers in six cities combined brain scans, psychological profiles, medical exams, and intelligence tests gathered from hundreds of apparently healthy children to attempt to determine what is "normal" in brain development (Hotz, 2007). Research about the brains of young people with psychiatric/behavioral disorders also appears very exciting. New, specific, genetic studies and new, specific, preventive measures, as well as new treatments after diagnoses have been made, are appearing on the horizon. We must remember, however, that, unfortunately, there is no "magic bullet"—these conditions are complex both in etiology and treatment. Hopefully, we soon will not need to wait until serious symptoms develop before we have multi-faceted programs to offer children, their families, and all of us who work with them.

Helping Children Achieve Their Potential

In 2006, the American Academy of Pediatrics published *A Parent's Guide to Building Resilience in Children and Teens: Giving Your Child Roots and Wings* (Ginsburg, 2006), which should help parents and others who work with children start early with helping children develop to their full potential.

Greenspan and Wieder (2007) discuss at length ways to work with children as early as possible. They advocate using techniques like "floor time" for parents to use to help their children communicate, as well as extensively using professionals like occupational and speech professionals.

Increased Vulnerability of Certain Groups of Children

While children of any economic level may have problems with mental health/behavioral conditions, some groups seem particularly vulnerable by way of "nurture" issues. Research is emerging that shows that significant numbers of formerly homeless families residing in permanent supportive housing have caregivers with substance use and mental health disorders and children with histories of exposure to violence, abuse, and out-of-home placement. Since these factors place young people at risk for adverse psychosocial outcomes, logically, child-focused prevention and intervention services should be developed in supportive housing contexts. One developing community-university partnership is presently underway whose goal is to advance practice and research in the adaptation and dissemination of mental illness prevention and early intervention for children in supportive housing (Gewirtz, 2007). The results hopefully will be helpful for children in other settings.

Children in foster care have social and emotional problems at rates three to ten times higher than those found in the general population. A pilot study from the University of Rochester, utilizing an existing evidenced-based intervention (the *Incredible Years*, developed for birth families) for foster caregivers, found that symptoms were significantly lower for children whose foster caregivers participated in the treatment group (Nilsen, 2007).

The Effect of Timing of the Trauma

While for some time experts have postulated maltreated children have a greater risk for poor psychological functioning in adulthood than those maltreated later in life, Kaplow and Widom (2007) tested this hypothesis. They looked at age of onset of maltreatment in three groups: a) continuous (ages 0-11 years), b) dichotomous (early [0-5 years] vs. later [ages 6-11 years]), and c) developmental (infancy, preschool, early school ages, and school age) . They found that an earlier onset predicted more symptoms of anxiety and depression in adulthood, even when controlled for gender, race, current age, and other reports of abuse. Later onset of maltreatment was predictive of more behavioral problems in adulthood.

CHAPTER 2

MOOD DISORDERS: DEPRESSION

Mood disorders are relatively common conditions that have as their main feature a disturbance in feeling. Mood disorders are divided into depressive disorders, bipolar disorders, and two disorders based on cause—general medical condition or substance-induced. This chapter discusses depressive disorders and Chapter 3 discusses bipolar disorders.

Prevalence

Depression Is Very Common

Depression is a very common type of mental illness, affecting millions of people in the United States and the rest of the world every year. Major depression is one of the most common conditions that primary care physicians are asked to diagnose and treat (Vollmer, 2002), representing the second most common chronic disorder seen in primary care offices (Sharp & Lipsky, 2002). In a study of prevalence of depressive symptoms in primary care medical practice, Zung, Broadhead, and Roth (1993) collected data from a sample of over 75,000 persons who visited the offices of 765 primary care physicians for any reason from February to September, 1991. They used an outcome measurement of the index score for the presence of depressive symptoms on the Zung Self-rating Depression Scale. The overall prevalence of significant symptoms of depression was 20.9%, but less than two percent of the individuals cited depression as the reason for their office visit. Rowe and his group (1995) studied 1898 patients from 88 primary care practices, using a self-administered health-habits questionnaire. They assessed depression both for lifetime incidence and for the past 30 days, using *Diagnostic and Statistical Manual of Mental Disorders, 3rd Edition Revised (DSM-*

III-R) (American Psychiatric Association, 1987) criteria for depression. Lifetime rates of depression were 36.1% for women and 23.3% for men.

Prevalence in Persons with ID

Many Individuals with ID Have Additional Psychiatric Diagnoses

A few isolated researchers have felt that their data show that depression occurs at lower rates in individuals with ID than in the general population (McDermott, Platt, & Krishnaswami, 1997), but most experts in the field do not agree. A fairly recent (2003) chapter in a textbook of clinical psychiatry reports a two- to four-fold increase in psychopathology, particularly depression, among persons with ID (Popper, Gammon, West, & Bailey, 2003). This text notes that fully half of people with ID have an additional psychiatric diagnosis, and psychiatric co-morbidity seems to increase with the severity of their impairment. The frequency in their assessment sample seems to be the same in both children and adults but probably is based on a referral population, which would be expected to show increased rates over the population with ID in general.

Lack of Discussion and Need for Systematic Investigation

After noting the occurrence of severe depressive reactions in people with ID, Gardner (1967) reviewed studies of the incidence of vulnerability of these individuals to severe depressive reactions. His reviews revealed little or no definitive data, and he felt that many studies had obvious defects. He stressed the need for systematic investigation of these issues. In another early study, Berman (1967) noted that depression seemed to be associated with aversive antisocial behavior in some individuals with developmental disabilities. Berman also noted the lack of discussion in the literature about the "depressed population" of people with ID. He felt this should be corrected to place the behavior in a more dynamic and therapeutically amenable light.

High Rate of Depression Among Adults with Mild ID

Prout and Schaefer (1985) administered three self-report measures of depression to adults with ID who lived in the community. They found the instruments to be significantly correlated, and on two of the measures the subjects scored significantly higher than did adults who do not have ID according to norms. Almost half of the subjects scored in the "clinically significant" range on those two measures. The authors note that their results suggest that adults with mild ID may experience depression at a higher rate than do persons without ID.

People with ID Manifest Full Range of Affective Disorders

Sovner and Hurley (1983) reviewed 25 published reports regarding the occurrence of affective illness, both depression and mania, in people with ID, using *DSM-III* criteria to assess the validity of both diagnoses. People with ID were found to manifest the full range of affective disorders. Developmentally impaired social functioning and intelligence influenced the clinical presentation, but not the development, of affective symptomatology. They note that these diagnoses can be made, even in people with severe/profound levels of ID and/ or those without language, by extended observations of behavior and vegetative functioning, including levels of motor activity, length and pattern of sleep, appetite and weight, and family historical data.

Underreporting of Incidence

More recently, Davis, Judd and Herrman (1997) examined the available literature regarding prevalence, clinical features and treatment of depression in adults with ID, both in community and hospital-based studies. They noted that few methodologically sound studies of prevalence had been reported. The clinical features of depression in adults with ID appears to vary with level of disability. They also note that prevalence rates of depression in individuals with ID appears to be underestimated due to problems in diagnosing depression in individuals who, characteristically, have communication problems. They concluded that well-designed studies to assess prevalence and evaluate treatment of depression in this group are urgently needed.

Prevalence in Older Adults

Patel, Goldberg, and Moss (1993) looked at the prevalence of psychiatric morbidity in 105 people over 50 years of age with learning disability, using the PASS-ADD. They found a prevalence excluding dementia of 11.4% (n = 12), most of which were depression and anxiety disorders. Seventy-five percent of these cases were unknown to mental health services. Immediate care staff were usually aware of the symptoms but were often unaware of their clinical significance. In another study from the United Kingdom, Cooper (1997) looked at the incidence of psychiatric disorders in aging people with developmental disabilities as compared with young adults from the same population. Elderly people had a greater prevalence of psychiatric morbidity than younger controls (68.7 v. 47.9%), with high rates for depression and anxiety disorder. Cooper made the point that as people with developmental disabilities age, their need for psychiatric services increases.

Epilepsy and Depression

Fairly recent reports (Kirn, 2003, Feb. 15) note the frequent occurrence of depression in people with epilepsy. Survey data suggest that major depression is more prevalent among people with epilepsy than among people with a non-neurologic chronic condition. Also, a PET study of patients with epilepsy detected temporal lobe dysfunction in association with depression. This would seem to be significant for a population of both children and adults with ID, with their relatively high incidence of associated epilepsy.

Diagnostic Criteria

A total of eight criteria for a major depressive episode are listed in *Diagnostic and Statistical Manual of Mental Disorders, 4th Edition, Text Revision* (*DSM-IV-TR*) (American Psychiatric Association, 2000), from which at least five must have been present during the same 2-week period and represent a change from previous functioning. ICD-10 criteria are similar. At least one of the symptoms must be depressed mood or loss of interest or pleasure in daily activities.

Depressed mood may be determined either by reports from the person himself/herself or from observations made by others. In children and adolescents, and persons with ID, the mood may be irritable rather than obviously depressed (Sovner & Fogelman, 1996). Depressed mood in a person with ID may also show up as a sad facial expression, withdrawal, vague physical complaints, onset of aggressive symptoms, and/or regression in behavior.

Weight Loss and Weight Gain

Other possible symptoms of depression include significant weight loss or weight gain, when not dieting, of five percent or more of body weight in a one-month period, or decrease or increase of appetite almost every day. Children with depression may not lose weight, but may fail to make expected weight gains for their gains in height. Their body mass index, weight in kilograms divided by the square of their height in meters, will therefore decrease. Changes in vital functions such as a decrease in appetite or insomnia are frequently the first manifestation of a mood disorder in adolescents with ID (Masi, 1998).

Diagnosing Depression in Individuals with ID

In the *Diagnostic Manual—Intellectual Disability* (*DM-ID*) chapter on mood disorders (Charlot et al., 2007), a number of points are made to facilitate diagnosis in this population. Developmental effects account for many of the variations in the clinical picture in people with ID, making careful collection of information about the person's behavior before the onset of psychiatric symptoms especially important. The authors of this chapter warn that although behavioral descriptions can be useful, the use of symptom substitutes should usually be avoided. As an example, if the individual is aggressive, this may be a "final common pathway" for a number of causes of personal distress. In an oral presentation at a national meeting of the National Association for the Dually Diagnosed (NADD) in 1990, Dr. Robert Sovner listed five causes of psychopathology for any given behavioral change, such as increased aggression: a) learned maladaptive behavior, b) central nervous system dysfunction, c) childhood onset pervasive developmental disorder, d) classic psychiatric disorder, and

e) medical/drug-induced disorder. None of these are mutually exclusive for any given behavior.

Childhood and Adolescence Issues

Heavy Supervision May Reduce Aggressive Behavior without Reducing the Rates of Depression and Anxiety

Kroll et al. (2002) assessed the mental health needs of 97 children and adolescent boys in secure care for serious or persistent offending. Twenty six (27.5%) of the boys had an intelligence quotient (I.Q.) of less than 70. The need for psychiatric help was high on admission to a secure unit, with the most frequent disorders being depression and anxiety. There were, of course, high rates of aggression, substance misuse, self-harm, and social, family and educational problems. The incidence of aggressive behavior and related problems decreased after admission because of the heavy supervision, but the rates of depression and anxiety remained high. The authors noted that many of these boys appeared to require psychiatric and psychological assessment, but this was done for only a small percentage.

Emotionally Disturbed Children and Depression

Twenty years ago Matson, Barrett, and Helsel (1988) looked at a group of 31 emotionally disturbed hospitalized children matched with a group of 31 children from a normal school setting and screened both groups for depression using the Child Depression Inventory and the Child Behavior Profile. Symptoms of depression were more prevalent in the children with ID. There were no significant gender or age differences, but the degree of overall psychopathology and depression were highly related. Data analysis suggested that similarities exist between depression in children with ID and those without such cognitive handicaps.

Seasonal Affective Disorder

Seasonal affective disorder is now a well-recognized variant of recurrent depressive disorder, where symptoms usually occur at a specific season of the year. Very little is known about the occurrence of this condition in people with ID. Cooke and Thompson (1998) reported two case histories in people with ID that showed good response to light therapy. They recommended that further studies should be done in this population, including standardized diagnostic criteria and systematic severity of depression scores. The incidence of this disorder in children, both with and without ID, is essentially unknown, but apparently it does occur.

The Effect of Sensory Impairments

Carvill (2001), looking at the coexistence of sensory impairments, ID, and psychiatric problems, noted that most studies agree that behavioral and developmental problems are more common among children who are blind or visually impaired, and probably among those who have hearing problems. Carvill notes that psychiatric assessment of individuals with sensory impairments is seldom easy and is especially difficult in those with ID. When no communication skills are present, careful and close observation of behavioral manifestations may be the only means of examination, but the examiner should be aware of the mannerisms and stereotypies often seen in individuals who are blind and those who are both blind and deaf.

Sleep Disorders

People of all ages with depression often have sleep disorders— either insomnia or hypersomnia (too little or too much sleep). Sleep disturbances in people with ID who are depressed may show up as disruptive behavior at bedtime or during the night, or as excessive sleepiness during daytime activities. Note should be made that individuals who are totally blind have a relatively high incidence of sleep disorders due to difficulty with entrainment (adjustment) to a 24-hour day. This is a particular issue in those blind people who have ID (Poindexter, 2002), so use of sleep disorder as a criterion for depression in an individual who has ID and total blindness may not be valid.

In another issue related to sleep and depression, a 2003 news article ("Clinical capsules") noted that children with epilepsy have a higher than normal rate of sleep apnea, and the apnea appears to be associated with mood and behavior disturbances. Since a significant percentage of children with ID have epilepsy, they may be more likely to experience apnea and related mood and behavior disturbances. In a survey of 23 children with epilepsy with an average age of 10 years, 19 had abnormal polysomnographs with obstructive hypopneas or apneas that disrupted sleep and caused hypoxia. A statistical analysis showed a clear relation between higher scores on measurements of hyperactivity-impulsive/inattentive behavior and delayed REM sleep onset. Also, higher scores on measures of depression were related to increased length of apnea intervals.

Psychomotor Agitation and Psychomotor Retardation

People of all ages with depression may be noted to have either psychomotor agitation or psychomotor retardation nearly every day, as observed by others. In different cultures depression may be masked by different acting-out behaviors representing psychomotor agitation. Both type and frequency are colored by local customs and determinants (Lesse, 1979). Psychomotor agitation in any person with ID may present as a behavior problem of recent onset, and psychomotor retardation may present as a change in productivity or performance in school or at work site. People with depression often complain of being tired or having a loss of energy.

Social Skills, Social Comparison, and Depression

Benson and her group (1985) studied psychosocial correlates of depression in adults with ID and found that depression was associated with informant ratings of poor social skills. Laman and Reiss (1987) identified specific social skill deficiencies associated with depressed mood in a group of 45 adults with ID who had mixed or no psychiatric diagnoses. They note that the subjects with depressed mood were withdrawn and interacted less with others and that their social interactions were more inappropriate and ineffective. They suggest that some instances of antisocial behavior might be motivated by depressed mood. Social comparison, the process by which we evaluate ourselves through comparison with others, is a cognitive process involved with mediation of depression. Helsel and

Matson (1988) studied a group of 99 adults with mild to severe ID on a variety of measures, and found that depression and social skill measures correlated significantly with each other on self-report and informant reports.

Manikam and his group (1995) administered self-report measures of depression, general psychopathology, and social skills to adolescents ranging from moderate ID to above normal intelligence. Adolescents with ID reported more depression and general psychopathology symptoms than did the cognitively normal control group. Adaptive behavior functioned as a moderator variable that mediated the relationship between depression and intellectual functioning. Dagnan and Sandhu (1999) looked at the relationship between social comparison processes, self-esteem, and depression in 43 people with mild and moderate ID, including young people. In their study, depression was significantly negatively correlated with social comparison on the social attractiveness and group-belonging dimensions and with positive self-esteem. Knowledge of these processes might improve cognitive behavioral interventions for this group of people.

Feelings of Worthlessness or Excessive Guilt

Individuals with depression often complain of feelings of worthlessness or excessive, inappropriate guilt. This guilt may be as extreme as being delusional and does not, by definition, involve merely self-reproach about being sick. Persons with ID who are depressed may express these feelings in statements such as "I'm dumb—stupid—no one likes me—" (Sovner, Hurley, & LaBrie, 1982). They may also have decreased ability to think or concentrate and may appear more indecisive than usual. These symptoms may be reported by the individual or by others. In people with ID, cognitive disturbances associated with depression may show up as a decrease in I.Q. or functional ability when retested or by change in attention span while performing their usual activities.

Suicide

People with depression, including adolescents and those with ID, often have recurrent thoughts of death or dying and may either think a lot about suicide, plan suicide, or make suicide attempts (Hurley, 1998; Patja, Livanainen, Raitasuo, & Lonnqvist, 2001). Patja's group (2001) noted that most of these suicide victims had mild ID and were hospitalized for co-morbid mental conditions. The suicide rate was about one third that of the rate in the general population with similar risk factors, and suicide methods were passive. Alcohol was involved in only one case.

The rate of suicides among young people aged 10 to 24 increased by eight percent from 2003 to 2004, to a total of nearly 4,600 deaths in the U.S. According to the CDC, suicides among girls aged 10 to 14 increased by 76%. Suicides were up 32% among girls 15 to 19 and 9% among boys aged 15 to 19. The suicide rate dropped 19% from 1990 to 2003 before the sharp increase in 2004, which was the most recent year data were collected. Some experts feel that the increase is at least partially due to "black box" warnings for antidepressant drugs which resulted in decreased prescribing of these medications. Probably some subgroups of patients became more suicidal when given antidepressants, as compared to the larger population ("Youth Suicides," 2007).

Social/Environmental Factors

Issues of diagnosis of psychiatric disorders in children and adolescents with specific social/environmental characteristics seem to be exceptionally significant. In a study examining factors related to psychiatric hospital readmission among children and adolescents who were wards of a midwestern state, Romansky, Lyons, Lehner, and West (2003) found that children who were readmitted within three months of discharge from the index hospitalization were significantly different in a number of ways from the children who were not readmitted. The former group was rated as more learning disabled or developmentally delayed and had received fewer post-hospital service hours than the group of children who were not readmitted. The highest rates of readmission were found among children who lived in congregate care settings before the index hospitalization and those who lived in a rural region. The authors note that these findings indicate that prevention of readmission among these children must focus on community-based services.

Nature and Nurture Factors: Life Events and Biological Causes

While depression presently is considered at least partially of biologic origin ("nature"), life events certainly still play a part in the development of the condition ("nurture") (Dubovsky, Davies, & Dubovsky, 2003). Basic epidemiologic and clinical research indicates that increased risk for depression in individuals of all ages is associated with being female, a family history of depression (particularly in a parent), sub-clinical (more mild) depressive symptoms, anxiety, stressful life events, negative thoughts, problems in self-regulation and coping with life, and interpersonal problems. All of these things both increase the person's chance of encountering stress and decrease their ability to deal with stress when it occurs (Garber, 2006).

Ghaziuddin and his group (1995) studied the role of life events in the occurrence of depression in a group of children with pervasive developmental disorders (PDD) and diagnosed depression as compared with a group of children with PDD and no diagnosed depression. Information was gathered about the occurrence of unpleasant life events in the 12 months prior to the onset of depression and from a comparable time period in the control group. Children with depression experienced significantly more unpleasant life events, particularly bereavement. The authors strongly urge that future studies include exploration of the role of both biologic factors and environmental stressors in the onset of depression in this population.

Effect of Maternal Depression on Children

Many women with depression have a history of antisocial behavior, but research into maternal depression in the past did not ascertain if this had implications for their children. Kim-Cohen, Caspi, Rutter, Tomas, and Moffitt (2006) in the Environmental Risk Longitudinal Twin Study looked at a nationally representative group of 1,106 families in which mothers were administered the Diagnostic Interview Schedule for Major Depressive Disorder and interviewed about their lifetime history of antisocial personality disorder symptoms. Mothers and teachers provided information regarding the children's behavior problems at five and seven years of age, and the authors assessed the quality of the caregiving environment through maternal reports and interviewer observations. They found that, when compared with children of mothers with depression only, the children of depressed and antisocial mothers had significantly higher levels of antisocial behavior and rates of *DSM-IV* conduct disorder, even after control for numbers of symptoms and chronicity of maternal major depressive disorder. The children of depressed and antisocial mothers were at an elevated risk of experiencing multiple caregiving abuses, including physical maltreatment, high levels of maternal hostility, and exposure to domestic violence. This seems to indicate that this would be an appropriate population for early intervention practices.

Intellectual Disability Issues

Depression and Developmental Disabilities

It is more than forty years since Gardner (1967) and Berman (1967) began to alert the field of developmental disability to the significance of depression in the developmental disability population being served, and much is left to be done. McBrien (2003) reports that the validity of the conceptual frameworks for depression is still in doubt, despite the present widespread acceptance that depression can occur in adults with ID. She notes that difficulties encountered in its assessment and diagnosis have hampered the individual clinician, leaving questions of prevalence, treatment choice, and outcome to remain problematic.

Assessing Individuals with ID

Depression is not easy to diagnose in many persons with ID, particularly those whose cognitive ability is within the severe or profound levels, primarily because of their inability to verbally express their feelings. Sovner and Hurley (1989) note that a clinical interview alone is rarely diagnostic. They feel that the diagnostic process cannot usually rely solely on the interview, but an assessment process must include detailed behavioral observations collected by family members, other caregivers, and workshop personnel. This is particularly important in assessing sleep disturbances and changes in performance. Psychiatric assessment of individuals with even profound ID can be carried out if longitudinal behavioral data have been collected on the basis of objective measurements of changes in mood and thinking. Charlot and her group (1993) surveyed two groups of institutionalized adults with ID, one group with a prior diagnosis of affective disorder and one with a prior diagnosis of another psychiatric disorder. They found that 13% of those in the affective disorder diagnosis group did not meet *DSM-III-R* criteria for depression or mania, but 20% of the other group did. Aggression was a frequent attendant of psychopathology in both groups. They felt that their findings supported previous reports that affective disorders may be under-diagnosed in this population, whether in adults or young people. Note should be made that most (74%) of the subjects in their survey had severe to profound ID.

Considerable disagreement often exists between information obtained from affected individuals themselves and other informants (Moss, Prosser, Ibbotson, and Goldberg, 1996). This clearly indicates the importance of interviewing both affected individuals and others to improve the sensitivity of case detection.

A fairly recently published practice guideline for assessment and diagnosis of mental health problems in adults with ID (Deb, Matthews, Holt, & Bouras, 2001) may be of great help in working out some of the diagnostic difficulties related to depression. The authors clearly describe clinical features, biologic features, cognitive features, appearance, and the psychotic features of severe cases. They outline guidelines for diagnosis and differential diagnosis, and they include an extensive evidence-based reference list.

Association Between Various Assessment Methods

Rojahn and his group (1994) investigated the association between various depression assessment methods in 38 adults with mild or moderate ID, half of whom had relatively high and the other half had relatively low depression screening scores. Utilizing measures which included a standard psychiatric interview, an informant rating scale, and a self-report measure, they found that association between measures was generally low, yielding discordant classification results.

Meyers (1998) examined the symptomatology of 28 people with severe depression with moderate to profound levels of ID. Seventeen of 28 manifested five or more criteria for major depression, as classified by *DSM-IV*. The mean number of criteria met for major depression was 4.6, with 5.2 criteria met for the 15 individuals with moderate ID. This was significantly greater than 3.8 criteria met for the 13 individuals with severe and profound ID. Other symptoms included aggression, self-injury, and stripping behavior, which occurred in 40% with moderate and 54% with severe/profound ID. Meyers reported that all of the 28 cases responded to antidepressant drugs and/or mood stabilizers.

Modified Criteria

Clarke and Gomez (1999) assessed the utility of modified DCR-10 criteria in the diagnosis of depression in a retrospective study of 11 inpatients with ID. Modifications to DCR-10 criteria were made by adding items found in earlier research to be behavioral equivalents of depression in people with severe ID. All of the 11 individuals had a remission of symptoms as described by the modified criteria within five weeks of starting antidepressant treatment. They point out the limitations of their study in that the study group was relatively small, other medications were being administered that may have influenced the mental state, and it is difficult to relate improvements seen with the prescription of an antidepressant medication to an actual diagnosis of depressive disorder.

Diagnostic Overshadowing

Lowry (1998) noted that many factors can interfere with the diagnosis of mood disorders in people with ID. Diagnostic overshadowing is the tendency of mental health clinicians and others to attribute any signs of psychopathology to the person's ID rather than a co-existing mental health problem (Reiss & Szysko, 1983). As a result, treatment programs may be slanted toward providing behavioral treatments and only considering psychiatric care if many of these interventions have failed. Even when access to psychiatric care is readily available, excessive use of antipsychotic medication in this population may mask underlying symptoms of mood disorders. These types of diagnostic issues may be quite significant in children and adolescents.

Diagnostic Instruments

Dexamethasone Suppression Test (DST)

Unfortunately, no valid laboratory test or other similar diagnostic procedure is currently available for the diagnosis of depression. Severe depression has been associated with an over-secretion of the hormone cortisol and possibly a loss of the normal daily rhythm variation of cortisol secretion. Assessment of cortisol patterns via the dexamethasone suppression test (DST) has been one of the most extensively investigated neuroendocrine challenge tests used in psychiatric research. Despite many studies, the role of the DST in clinical psychiatry is unclear (Morihisa, Cross, Price, Precioso, & Koontz, 2003). Mattes and Amsell (1993) performed the DST for three groups of institutionalized persons with ID. The groups included persons with symptoms of depression, nondepressed persons with other problematic behavior, and control subjects. Results showed that depressed individuals more frequently, though not significantly, had positive DST tests compared with the other two groups. The group with problematic behaviors did not differ from the control group. Note should be made that in this study no mention is made about whether any of the persons in any group was receiving anticonvulsant drugs such as phenytoin, carbamazepine, or barbiturates, since these drugs, as well as a number of medical conditions, interfere significantly with the DST (Morihisa et al., 2003). Mudford et al. (1995) administered the DST to 40 adults with severe and profound ID. All participants were free from known conditions that may have given misleading results. Of nine participants who showed symptoms possibly indicating depression, the DST results concurred in two cases. However, there appeared to be four or five false-positive DST results, and no consistent behavioral profile was evident for positive DST responders. This group of researchers notes that their data do not suggest usefulness for the DST in this population.

Psychopathology Instrument for Mentally Retarded Adults (PIRMA)

A number of instruments have been designed over the years to assess depression and other psychiatric disorders in persons with developmental disabilities. While many of these instruments primarily were tested on adults, they probably have value in younger persons also. In 1983, Kazdin, Matson, and Senatore assessed 110 adults with borderline, mild, moderate, or severe ID, utilizing a number of tests. The test battery included modified versions of the Beck Depression Inventory, the Zung Self-Rating Depression Scale, the MMPI depression scale, the Thematic Apperception Test, and the Psychopathology Instrument for Mentally Retarded Adults (PIMRA). Both clinical and direct service personnel rated the individuals on the Hamilton Rating Scale for Depression and an informant version of the PIMRA. They found that the measures correlated significantly with each other and were consistently related to the diagnosis of depression. Matson, Kazdin, and Senatore (1984) examined the psychometric properties of the PIMRA in 110 adults with ID ranging from borderline to severe levels. The psychometric properties of the scale were reviewed and/or evaluated, including internal consistency of items, test-retest reliability, and factor analysis. Balboni, Battagliese, and Pedrabissi (2000) investigated whether the PIMRA (Senatore, Matson, & Kazdin, 1985) could detect specific psychopathological disorders in 652 individuals with ID living in the community or in residential facilities. The sample included people with different levels of ID. As a part of their study they compared 55 persons with anxiety disorders and 49 with depression to 50 control subjects of the same age, intelligence level, and gender ratio but without dual diagnosis. Those with diagnoses had higher factorial scores, both on the overall scale and on the factors specifically related to their disorders.

Self-Report Depression Questionnaire (SRDQ)

Reynolds and Baker (1988) looked at the psychometric characteristics of the Self-Report Depression Questionnaire (SRDQ), a 32-item self-report measure of depressive symptomatology in persons with ID, in a group of 89 adults living in community-based settings. While they felt that their results were positive, they pointed out that they should be viewed as one of several assessment perspectives that might provide valuable insight regarding affective status of people with ID. They also noted that the SRDQ is not a diagnostic instrument; it doesn't provide a formal diagnosis of depression.

Psychometric Perspective

Sturmey, Reed, and Corbett (1991) critically reviewed a group of instruments used for possible diagnosis of depression from a psychometric perspective. They found that although some psychometrically sophisticated measures were identified, the area was marked by an absence of important psychometric data for many measures. They note that the period of the 80's was marked by considerable research into the development of assessments of psychopathology in people with learning difficulties, but much of this research was of a preliminary nature and required further development and refinement. They felt that further research should be done both for development and validation of screening procedure and instrument formats, and that further studies should include more individuals with severe and profound learning difficulties.

Reiss Screen for Maladaptive Behavior

Reiss and Rojahn (1993) looked at the relationship between aggression and depression in 528 adults, adolescents, and children, who were rated on either the adult or child versions of the Reiss assessment instruments for dual diagnosis (Reiss, 1988; Reiss & Valenti-Hein, 1990). Criterion levels of depression were evident in about four times as many aggressive as nonaggressive subjects. The authors note that aggression is sometimes associated with syndromes of psychopathology other than depression, as mentioned earlier. They suggest that by evaluating when aggression is and is not associated with various categories of psychopathology, future researchers may be in a position to find ways of improving the effectiveness of clinical treatment—as in prescribing medications specifically for the underlying diagnosis rather than just for the aggression itself. Very recently, Gustafsson and Sonnander (2002) performed a psychometric evaluation of a Swedish version of the Reiss Screen for Maladaptive Behavior and noted that this instrument can be used as intended by staff members as a primary screening device for the identification of mental health problems in people with ID in a Swedish setting.

The Children's Depression Inventory, the Bellevue Index of Depression, and the Reynolds Child Depression Scale

Benavidez and Matson (1993) investigated the performance of 25 adolescents with mild to severe ID and 25 adolescents with normal intelligence on self-report and informant versions of three childhood depression measures, the Children's Depression Inventory, the Bellevue Index of Depression, and the Reynolds Child Depression Scale. Strong correlations between total measure scores were found. Analyses of variance comparing adolescents with ID and the control group differed significantly only on the Bellevue Index of Depression. The relationship between self-report and informant versions were correlated with mixed results.

Self-Reports About Feelings and Emotions from Individuals with ID

The consistency of reports about feelings and emotions from individuals with ID was assessed by Lindsay, Michie, Baty, Smith, and Miller (1994) in a group of 65 people with mild or moderate ID. All of the measures were self-report measures. The test battery included the Zung Self-Rating Anxiety Scale, the Zung Depression Inventory, the General Health Questionnaire, and the Eysenck-Withers Personality Test. Results showed a significant amount of convergent validity in the subjects' emotional systems.

Psychiatric Assessment Schedule for Adults with Developmental Disability (PASS-ADD) and Mini PASS-ADD

Groups of investigators from the United Kingdom have performed a number of studies on the Psychiatric Assessment Schedule for Adults with Developmental Disability (PASS-ADD) and Mini PASS-ADD instruments. Moss, Prosser, Ibbotson, and Goldberg (1997) investigated the ability of the PASS-ADD to detect symptoms that had been found to exist during routine clinical assessment of individuals. They found that this instrument was in good agreement with the information provided by referring psychiatrists. The Mini PASS-ADD was developed to enable non-psychiatrists to accurately recognize clinically significant psychiatric disorders in the people they serve. Prosser and his group (1998) investigated the internal consistency, inter-rater agreement, and validity in relation to clinical opinion, using a sample of 68 people with ID who were in contact with psychiatric services. The validity results (81% agreement on case recognition) appeared to be sufficiently good to anticipate that this instrument will be helpful. Deb, Thomas, and Bright (2001) used the Mini PASS-ADD to screen for presence of psychiatric disorders in 101 randomly selected adults with ID and the people who care for them. Out of this group 90 had sufficient communicative abilities to make the administration of the test possible. The full PASS-ADD was then used for psychiatric interviews in 20 individuals who were picked up on the original screening by an interviewer blind to the original results. Final diagnosis was made according to ICD-10 criteria. Three individuals were felt to have depression on the initial screening (3.3%) and two were felt to have depression after full testing (2.2%). These figures were roughly comparable to percentages in other studies. Feasibility, reliability, and validity of the Spanish version of PASS-ADD (PAS-ADD-10) was assessed by Gonzalez-Gordon, Salvador-Carulla, Romero, Gonzalez-Saiz, and Romero in 2002. They felt that its overall feasibility was judged adequate by raters, and was considered extremely useful for training.

Checklist of Challenging Behavior (CCB)

Utilizing the Checklist of Challenging Behavior (CCB), Jenkins et al. (1998) surveyed the prevalence of challenging behavior in a group of 63 individuals with difficult behavior, utilizing the PIMRA, observer version, for comparison. The relationship between non-aggressive behaviors as measured by the CCB and mental health as measured by the PIMRA showed significant overlap, but there was less consistency in the relationship between aggressive behaviors in the CCB and the PIMRA. They felt that their study confirmed the difficulties in discriminating between challenging behavior (probably learned maladaptive behavior) and behavior resulting from the presence of mental health problems.

Children's Depression Inventory (CDI)

Ailey (2000) investigated the reliability and validity of the Children's Depression Inventory (CDI) using 27 adolescents with mild ID attending schools in a large metropolitan area. Scores on the self-report CDI were compared with scores on an observer-completed inventory of psychopathology, the Reiss Scales for Children's Dual Diagnosis, completed by teachers and other staff. For female students, statistically significant negative associations were found between CDI scores and scores on the Reiss Scales and its depression subscale. Note was made that school nurses may find the CDI useful as a self-report screening tool for depression.

Concurrent Validity of Different Informant and Self-Report Assessment Instruments

Masi, Brovedani, Mucci, and Favilla (2002) examined the concurrent validity of different informant and self-report assessment instruments of psychopathology, both general and specific for anxiety and/or depression, in referred adolescents with ID who were diagnosed with depression and/or anxiety disorders according to DSM-IV criteria. Their sample was a consecutive group of 50 adolescents with mild and moderate ID with a mean age of 15.1 years. They were assessed using standardized assessment techniques, including the PIMRA, informant version, total score, affective and anxiety subscales, Child Behavior Checklist (CBCL), informant version, total score, internalizing and externalizing scores, anxiety-depression scale, and Zung Self-Rating Depression and Anxiety Scales. PIMRA and CBCL total scores were closely intercorrelated. Anxiety measures were positively correlated, with PIMRA and CBCL total scores, as well as with the internalizing score of CBCL. Depression measures were not correlated with the other instruments, and their correlation with more general measures of psychopathology was weak.

Beck Depression Inventory and Zung Self Rating Scale

Psychometric properties of the Beck Depression Inventory and the Zung Self Rating Scale in adults with ID were recently reported by Powell (2003). His findings suggest that these tests have good clinical utility with adults with ID, and that depression in these individuals may be more severe than in others. The Beck Depression Inventory appeared to have clinical validity with this population, but the Zung scale may have had problems. Results also showed that there may be a tendency of these persons to minimize their distress, thus further complicating the diagnostic process.

Marston 30 Symptoms Checklist

Use of the DSM system (American Psychiatric Association, 1987; 2000) is fraught with many difficulties primarily because of communication problems with the affected individual, as mentioned earlier. Hurley explored major depressive episodes occurring in individuals with Down syndrome (1996) and described a framework for substituting "mental retardation equivalents" for standard diagnostic criteria. Tsiouris (2001) used the Marston 30 Symptoms Checklist to determine whether or not the notion of "depressive equivalents" could provide a few of the core characteristics needed for the diagnosis of depressive disorders in people with severe/profound ID. His study found that the first six observable criteria of *DSM-III-R*, including irritable mood, were sufficient for diagnosing major depression in people with severe/profound ID. He noted the particular importance of sleep and appetite disturbances and changes in the level of activity.

Prevention and Amelioration

A Family-Based Approach

Since depression in parents is common and children of depressed parents are at risk for psychopathology and other difficulties, Beardslee, Gladstone, Wright, and Cooper (2003) studied a family-based approach to the prevention of depressive symptoms in these children. They adopted a developmental perspective and intervened with families when children were entering adolescence, the age of highest risk for depression onset. They sought to reduce risk factors and enhance protective factors by increasing positive interactions between parents and children and by increasing understanding of the illness for everyone in the family. They enrolled families with relatively healthy children, administered carefully designed preventive interventions that are manual-based and relatively brief, and found that the programs had long-standing positive effects in how families problem solve around parental illness. No mention was made about whether or not the children involved had developmental disabilities.

Positive Social Supports

Early childhood maltreatment interacts with genetic susceptiblity to increase risk for psychopathology, but environmental factors can also have protective effects, even when the individuals has genetic susceptiblity. When such maltreated children have positive social supports, they have less risk of developing depression than children who do not have these supports (Smoller & Korf, 2008).

Culturally Sensitive Mental Health School-Based Program

Many southeast Asian refugee children have experienced a great deal of violence before coming to the United States and have high rates of depression and/or post-traumatic stress disorder. Fox, Rossetti, Burns, and Popovich (2005) provided an eight-week school-based program designed to reduce depression symptoms in these refugee children. All the children were screened for depression using the Children's Depression Inventory. Analysis of data revealed that children's depression scores had a significant decrease between screening times one (about one month before the intervention) and two (fourth week of the intervention), one and three (eighth week of the intervention) and one and four (one month following the intervention. The authors felt that culturally sensitive mental health school-based programs may be an appropriate intervention to assist immigrant and refugee children to successfully adapt to host countries.

A Manualized After-School Intervention

Children who exhibit elevated levels of conduct problems are at increased risk for developing co-occurring depression symptoms, especially during adolescence. Cutuli and his group (2006) looked at the effectiveness of a manualized after-school intervention for a set of middle-school-aged students with conduct problems but no depressive symptoms and found that the program successfully prevented elevations in depression symptoms compared to no-intervention controls.

Need for Further Research on Treatment for Individuals with ID

Despite the obvious high incidence of depression in populations of individuals with developmental disability and the frequent efficacy of treatment for the condition described in the general population, virtually nothing has been reported about treatment results in persons with developmental disability. This clearly seems to be an overlooked important research area, which hopefully will be soon addressed. In late 2001 a conference dealing with research on mental health problems in people with ID was held in Rockville, Maryland, sponsored by the National Institute of Neurological Disorders and Stroke (NINDS), the National Institute of Child Health and Human Development, the National Institute of Mental Health, the National Institutes of Health Office of Rare Diseases, and the Joseph P. Kennedy Jr. Foundation (National Institute of Neurological Disorders & Stroke, 2005). The workshop was designed to identify barriers to the inclusion of people with ID and developmental disabilities in federally funded research in the United States. The goal was to define ways to increase inclusion of people with ID in research in order to promote evidence-based treatment for this population. A copy of the actions of this conference can be obtained from the NINDS website. This certainly seems to be an important step forward in addressing the issues of clinical research in this population.

CHAPTER 3

MOOD DISORDERS: BIPOLAR DISORDER

Prevalence

Data on the prevalence of Bipolar I and Bipolar II disorder in the general population have not yet been outlined clearly, and prevalence data are almost non-existent for young people and those with ID.

Diagnostic Criteria

Bipolar I Diagnostic Criteria

Bipolar I disorder is marked by one or more episodes of mania or mixed episodes, and usually occurs alternating with major episodes of depression (Charlot et al., 2007). A manic episode is defined by a distinct period during which an abnormally and persistently elevated (euphoric), expansive, or irritable mood is present, lasting at least a week. The abnormal mood in a manic episode, according to *DSM-IV-TR*, must be accompanied by at least three other symptoms from a list which includes inflated self-esteem or boldness, decreased need for sleep, pressure of speech (very fast talking), flight of ideas, distractibility, increased involvement in goal-directed and/or pleasurable activities with high risk of bad outcomes, and agitation (American Psychiatric Association, 2000). The *DM-ID* does not suggest specific adaptations for using these criteria in persons with intellectual disability (Charlot et al., 2007).

Criteria for a Manic Episode

To be considered part of a manic episode, symptoms must be severe enough to cause marked impairment in social, occupational, or educational functioning and/or to require hospitalization. Elevated mood during a manic episode may be described as unusually good, cheerful, or "high." While elevated mood is a standard symptom of a manic episode, irritability or switching back and forth between euphoria and irritability is often seen, particularly when the person's wishes are not immediately carried out.

Inflated Self-Esteem

Inflated self-esteem is usually present. This can vary from uncritical self-confidence all the way to marked grandiosity, which may appear delusional. A person in a manic episode may feel extremely important and wise, and may give advice on matters about which he or she knows nothing. The person usually has a decreased need for sleep, often awakening several hours earlier than usual, feeling full of energy, and even may go for days without sleep, without feeling tired.

Pressured Speech and Racing Thoughts

Manic speech is usually pressured, loud, very rapid, and quite difficult to interrupt. The person may become theatrical, with dramatic gestures, joking, and singing. Sounds rather than meaning of words may govern word choice, a process known as *clanging*. A person in a manic episode may have racing thoughts as well as a great deal of distractibility—often resulting in a "flight of ideas," an almost continuous flow of fast speech, with sudden changes from one topic to another. Often the person's hyperactivity appears to be cyclic, but we need to remember that not all cyclic behavior patterns are bipolar disorder.

Bipolar II Diagnostic Criteria

Bipolar II disorder is marked by depressive episodes alternating with one or more hypomanic episodes, but not with full-blown mania. A hypomanic episode is one in which symptoms are not severe enough to cause marked functional impairment. A mixed episode is marked by a period of time, lasting at least one week, in which criteria are met both for a manic episode and a major depressive episode nearly every day, with rapid alternation of mood between the two extremes. The disturbance must be sufficiently severe to cause marked impairment in life and/or to require hospitalization.

Childhood and Adolescence Issues, Including Prevention and Amelioration

Bipolar Disorder and Children

Interest in bipolar disorder in children and adolescents has increased greatly in recent years. Faust, Walker, and Sands (2006) remind us that early-onset bipolar disorder is often misdiagnosed and inadequately treated because of the varying collection of symptoms that occur across different developmental stages, the variety of disorders with similar presentation, and the frequent comorbidities. Chang and his group (2006) note that bipolar disorder is a prevalent condition in the United States that typically begins before the age of 18 years and is being increasingly recognized in children and adolescents. Even with great efforts to discover more effective treatments, it remains a difficult-to-treat condition with high morbidity and mortality. They recommend the development of early interventions that may help delay the onset of the first manic episode and/or prevent development of full bipolar disorder. High risk populations include children with strong family histories of bipolar disorder who are experiencing symptoms of attention-deficit/hyperactive disorder (ADHD) and/or depression or have early mood dysregulation, since these children may be experiencing prodromal states of bipolar disorder. Rende et al. (2007) found childhood-onset bipolar disorder to be associated with an increased family psychiatric history when compared with adolescent-onset.

Age of Onset

Leverich et al. (2007) examined the age of onset of bipolar disorder as a possible course-of-illness modifier with the hypothesis that early onset will lead to more severe illness. They concluded that their data showed that childhood onset is common and is often associated with long delays to first treatment. They feel that early diagnosis and appropriate treatment may help ameliorate the otherwise adverse course of the condition. Masi et al. (2006) looked at a large sample of unselected, consecutive children and adolescents who received a diagnosis of bipolar disorder who were referred to a third-level hospital in Italy, checking to see whether childhood-onset, as compared with adolescent-onset, presents specific clinical features in terms of severity, functional impairment, course, prevalent mood, pattern of co-morbidity, and treatment outcome. Compared with adolescent-onset of the disorder, those with childhood-onset were more frequently males and had a more frequent co-morbidity with ADHD and oppositional defiant disorder. An episodic course was found in only 42.5% of bipolar children but was present in 76.8% of those with adolescent-onset. Severity, 6-month treatment outcome, prevalent mood, and co-morbid anxiety did not differ between the two groups. Masi and his group concluded that a very early age at onset may identify a form of bipolar disorder with a more frequent subcontinuous course and a heavy co-morbidity with ADHD.

Public Health Implications

Jolin, Weller, and Weller (2007) point out the public health aspects of bipolar disorder in children and adolescents. They feel this is a major public health problem associated with significant functional impairment, since these individuals are at increased risk for substance-related disorders, weight problems, and impaired social support systems.

Mania in Preschoolers

Luby, Tandon, and Nicol (2007) report three clinical cases of manic symptoms in preschoolers, ages 3.6 to 5.2, who were seen in a subspecialty mental health clinic with age-adjusted mania-like symptoms including grandiosity, hypersexuality, elation, racing thoughts, and decreased need for sleep. They note these symptoms are highly specific for distinguishing bipolar disorder from attention deficit hyperactivity disorder (ADHD) in older children. In a somewhat earlier study (2006), Luby and Belden looked at the clinical characteristics and adaptive functioning of preschoolers who met *DSM-IV* criteria for bipolar disorder versus psychiatric and healthy comparison groups. The two psychiatric groups were disruptive disorders and major depressive disorder. The children with bipolar disorder were clearly differentiated from the other two groups by way of a parent report of mania symptoms using an age-appropriate psychiatric interview. They felt that these children can be distinguished from healthy and disruptive disordered preschoolers.

Episode and Cycle

While the words "episode" and "cycle" were used interchangeably in the early adult bipolar literature and "rapid cycling" referred to multiple episodes per year, Geller et al. (2007) recommend the use of "episode" for the interval between onset and offset of full *DSM-IV* criteria for bipolar disorder and "cycling" only for daily switching of mood states that occurs during an episode instead of the use of "rapid cycling" with "multiple episodes per year." They feel that these clarifications will be very important for research in preschool populations.

Sleep Problems and Bipolar Disorders

Even though sleep problems are one of the diagnostic criteria for mood disorders, very little research has been reported on sleep difficulties in early-onset bipolar spectrum disorders. One study of a sample of 133 children ages 8 to 11 with this condition (Lofthouse, Fristad, Splaingard, & Kelleher, 2007) used both parental and self-report measures and found a high discrepancy between parent and child reports. Later analysis of data showed that a majority (96.2%) of the children had moderate to severe sleep problems, either currently or during their worst mood period. More depression-related sleep problems than mania-related sleep problems were reported, especially initial insomnia.

Children with ID and Bipolar Disorder

As noted earlier, virtually nothing has been reported about bipolar disorder in children with ID and/or autism spectrum disorders. Jan et al. (1994) described an incapacitating, regularly recurring, biphasic disorder in six children with severe multiple disabilities. This disorder was marked by several days of lethargy, withdrawal, loss of abilities, irritability, and hypersomnolence (excessive sleepiness), followed or preceded by a high-energy state for several days during which the children slept very little, at times were euphoric, had improved mental ability, and were hyperactive. These cyclic episodes had been present for years but unexpectedly disappeared in one child. The etiology was unknown, in spite of detailed neurologic, metabolic, and endocrine investigations. All had family histories positive for affective disorders. The authors felt that these children seemed to have a unique disorder that closely resembles or is a variant of rapid cycling affective disorder. More recent research would suggest that this is true.

CHAPTER 4

ANXIETY DISORDERS:
GENERAL INFORMATION

....

Prevalence

Anxiety disorders are the most common mental health disorders seen by primary care physicians. A primary care doctors probably sees at least one person with an anxiety disorder in his/her office every day (McGlynn & Metcalf, 1989). The characteristic features of this group of disorders include symptoms of anxiety and avoidance behavior.

Diagnostic Criteria

Panic Attack

A *panic attack* is not a diagnosis but a group of symptoms which occur in all kinds of anxiety disorders. This is a group of symptoms that occur during a discrete period of time, causing intense fear and/or discomfort. The *DSM-IV-TR* and *DM-ID* list 13 of these symptoms, four of which must be present, develop suddenly, and reach a peak within ten minutes: 1) palpitations; 2) sweating; 3) trembling or shaking; 4) shortness of breath or sensation of smothering; 5) feeling of choking; 6) chest pain or discomfort; 7) nausea or abdominal distress; 8) feeling dizzy or faint; 9) derealization (see below); 10) fear of losing control or "going crazy"; 11) fear of dying; 12) numbness or tingling sensations (parathesias); and 13) chills or hot flashes.

Generalized Anxiety Disorder

Many people with anxiety have *generalized anxiety disorder*, in which they have excessive anxiety and worry about a number of events or activities. For this to be diagnosable they must have symptoms more days than not for at least six months. The individual with generalized anxiety disorder finds it very hard to control his or her worry. Symptoms that may be associated with generalized anxiety disorder include restlessness, easy fatigability, trouble concentrating, irritability, muscle tension, and some sort of sleep disturbance, which may be trouble falling or staying asleep or restless, unsatisfying sleep. The anxiety, worry, and/or physical symptoms of generalized anxiety disorder cause clinically significant distress or impairment in social, occupational, or other important areas of functioning.

Agoraphobia

The term *agoraphobia* means anxiety about being in places or situations from which escape might be difficult or embarrassing, or in which help might not be available if an unexpected panic attack occurs. People who have agoraphobia may refuse to leave their home because of fear of a panic attack. To make a diagnosis of *panic disorder* with agoraphobia, the person must have recurrent, unexpected panic attacks. At least one attack should be followed by a month or more of persistent concern about having more attacks, worry about implications of the attack or its consequences, and/or a significant behavior change related to the attacks. Effects of some prescribed drugs, drugs of abuse, or over-active thyroid function may present with symptoms similar to those of a panic attack.

Depersonalization and Derealization

Another symptom often association with anxiety disorders is the feeling of detachment from all or parts of one's body—*depersonalization*. Sometimes people who have anxiety disorders also have the sensation that the immediate environment is strange, unreal, or unfamiliar—*derealization*.

Specific Phobia

A *specific phobia* is defined as a marked and persistent fear of a specific object or situation, such as fear of flying, heights, animals, receiving an injection ("shot"), and seeing blood. Exposure to the specific object or situation usually causes an immediate anxiety response, which often takes the form of a panic attack. In children, crying, tantrums, freezing, or clinging may express panic associated with a phobia. Persons with ID may react in a similar way or may become aggressive to get away from the feared situation. While adults with phobias usually recognize that the fear is excessive or unreasonable, children and those with ID may not do so. In a true phobia, by definition, the avoidance, anxious anticipation, or distress in the feared situations interferes significantly with normal routine, functioning, social activities, or relationships with others, or there is marked distress about having the problem.

Social Phobia

According to the *DSM-IV-TR*, *social phobia*, also known as social anxiety disorder, is a marked and persistent fear of social or performance situations in which embarrassment may occur. Exposure to these situations almost always provokes an immediate anxiety response, which may or may not be a panic attack.

Anxiety Disorders with Particular Issues in Young People

Distinguishing Anxiety from Depression

While depression and anxiety disorders have some symptoms in common, and may occur in the same person, the features more characteristic of anxiety include trouble falling asleep, avoidance behavior based on fear, rapid pulse, trouble breathing, fearfulness, tremors, heart palpitations, sweating, hot or cold spells, and dizziness. Sleep-related problems are particularly common in children with anxiety disorders and should be assessed for and tended to both in research and clinical settings (Alfano, Ginsburg, & Kingery, 2007).

Social Phobia and Childhood Experiences

Social anxiety disorder (social phobia) is among the most common mental disorders on a lifetime basis, ranging from 12% to 14% (Stein, 2006). In Sweden, Marteinsdottir et al. (2007) looked at the relationship between life events and social phobia, utilizing an inventory assessing life events during childhood and adulthood as well as life events experienced in relation to the onset of the disorder. They compared a group of 30 persons with a *DSM-IV* diagnosis of social phobia as compared to 75 controls selected by matching age and gender from the same local population. People with social phobia reported significantly more life events during childhood and more life events with negative impact during the year before the onset of the social phobia, but less events in adult life, than the controls.

The clinical picture and resulting problems in social phobia may differ across cultures, depending on social demands. In children, crying, tantrums, freezing, clinging, or staying close to a familiar person may be present, as well as inhibited interactions as extreme as mutism (refusal to speak). Children with social phobia usually can't avoid feared situations completely. There may be a decline in school performance, school refusal, and/or avoidance of age-appropriate social activities. To make the diagnosis in children, there must be evidence for capacity for social relationships with familiar people and the social anxiety must occur in peer settings, not just in interactions with adults. Because of the early onset of the disorder, children's impairment usually takes the form of failure to achieve an expected level of functioning, rather than a decline from an optimal level of functioning.

Impact of Nature and Nurture Upon Anxiety Disorders

Development of anxiety disorders in children is another example of the "nature plus nurture" conundrum. Biederman et al. (2006) looked at the association between anxiety disorders in parents and offspring in a sample of children at risk for panic disorder. They found that social phobia and separation anxiety disorder in the children were accounted for by the same disorders in the parent, whereas agoraphobia and obsessive-compulsive disorder in the children were accounted for by parental panic disorder.

Anxiety and School Refusal

In India, Prabhuswamy and his group (2007) looked at psychiatric diagnoses, psychosocial correlates, and short-term outcome of

33 children with school refusal and found that 87.9% had a psychiatric diagnosis—depressive disorder was most common, followed by specific phobias for about a third of those with a psychiatric diagnosis. Psychosocial factors influenced school refusal in almost eighty percent of the studied cases.

Need for Further Research

In a study examining the psychiatric histories of adults with anxiety disorders, looking at each type of anxiety disorders, about half with each type of anxiety disorder had been diagnosed with a psychiatric disorder by age 15. One-third of these were diagnosed with an anxiety disorder. Histories of anxiety and depression were most common. Adults with panic disorder did not have histories of juvenile disorders, whereas those with other anxiety disorders did. Adults with posttraumatic stress disorder had histories of conduct disorder, but those with other anxiety disorders did not. Adults with specific phobia had histories of juvenile phobias but not other anxiety disorders. The authors suggest that the early first diagnosis of psychiatric problems in people with anxiety disorders points out the need to target research about the etiology of anxiety disorders and prevention early in life (Gregory et al., 2007).

Prevention and Ameliorations

Educational Asistance and Social Skills Development

Meshane, Bazzano, Walter, and Barton (2007), working in Australia, evaluated the outcome of adolescents with anxiety-based school attendance problems enrolled in a specialist educational and mental health program that provides education assistance and social skills development. Their findings confirmed the effectiveness of, and need for, flexible programs to support adolescents with social anxiety disorder and other longer-term mental health problems to offset the adverse consequences of early withdrawal from educational and social environments.

CHAPTER 5

ANXIETY DISORDERS:
POST-TRAUMATIC STRESS DISORDER

Diagnostic Criteria

Re-Experiencing a Traumatic Event

Post-traumatic stress disorder (PTSD) is an anxiety disorder in which the involved person has been exposed to a traumatic event in which he or she has experienced, witnessed, or been confronted with a situation that involved actual or threatened death or serious injury to self or others, and the person's response involved intense fear, helplessness, or horror. Examples may include a person who comes close to death by fire or someone who has been sexually abused—either of these may develop PTSD. Also, in post-traumatic stress disorder the traumatic event is persistently re-experienced. This can happen in a variety of ways, including recurrent and intrusive recollections of the event ("flashbacks"); recurrent, distressing dreams of the event; acting or feeling as if the event were recurring; intense psychological distress to cues symbolizing the event (such as odors associated with event); and/or physical symptoms on exposure to cues of the event.

Avoidance and Detachment

People with PTSD have persistent avoidance of stimuli associated with the trauma and have numbing of general responsiveness. These symptoms may present as efforts to avoid thoughts, feelings, or conversations associated with the trauma, efforts to avoid situations or people that cause memories of the trauma, and/or inability to recall facts about the trauma. Other manifestations of PTSD may include a decreased interest or participation in significant activities, feelings of detachment or estrangement from others, inability to have loving feelings, and/or a sense of a foreshortened future—not expecting to have a normal life span.

Increased Arousal

Individuals with PTSD also have persistent symptoms of increased arousal, such as trouble falling or staying asleep, irritability or outbursts of anger, trouble concentrating, hypervigilance (always "on the lookout"), and/or exaggerated startle reflex. To make a diagnosis of post-traumatic stress disorder, the disturbance must cause clinically significant distress or impairment in important areas of functioning. Symptomatology is relatively consistent across all age groups.

Childhood and Adolescence Issues

Important to Directly Interview Children

A study from the United Kingdom looked at whether or not children and parents agreed on the presence of symptoms of acute stress disorder, PTSD, and other psychopathology after the children were exposed to single-event trauma, and found that children were significantly more likely to meet criteria for disorders based on their own report rather than on their parents' report. The authors point out that their findings support the need to directly interview children and adolescents for early screening efforts (Meiser-Stedman, Smith, Glucksman, Yule, & Dalgleish, 2007).

Fear Conditioning Shortly After Trauma

Bryant, Salmon, Sinclair, and Davidson (2007) looked at the relationship between resting heart rates after injury and subsequent post-traumatic stress disorder in children. Full PTSD or subsyndromal PTSD was diagnosed in 27% of 62 injured children. These children had higher heart rates after the trauma than those without PTSD, even after controlling for age, gender, and injury severity. The authors note that these findings go along with the proposal that fear conditioning shortly after trauma contributes to PTSD in children.

Childhood Factors That Increase Risk

Koenen et al. (2007) studied childhood factors that have been reported to be associated with increased risk of developing PTSD. They identified two sets of childhood risk factors. The first set, which included childhood externalizing characteristics and family environmental stressors, was associated with increased risk of trauma exposure and with PTSD at age 26. The second set of risk factors affected risk for PTSD only and included low I.Q. and chronic environmental adversity. The authors conclude that rather than being only a response to trauma, PTSD may have developmental origins—the "nature" factor again. Breslau, Lucia, and Alvarado (2006) used a prospective community study to look at early predispositions to development of PTSD and found that children with an I.Q. at age six of 115 or above had decreased risk for non-assaultive trauma and decreased conditional PTSD.

Witnessing Traumatic Events

A study was made of PTSD in 200 children aged 7-11 years who had witnessed a public hanging next to their school in Isfahan, Iran. Parents were interviewed with a standard checklist three months after the event. PTSD symptoms were identified in 104 children (52%) with 88 suffering re-experiences, 24 avoidance, and 62 hyperarousal. This study highlights the serious emotional effects on children who witness traumatic events (Attari, Dashty, & Mahmoodi, 2006).

Exposure to Catastrophic Events

In the general population of children, potentially traumatic events are fairly common and do not often result in PTSD symptoms except after multiple traumas or a history of anxiety (Copeland, Keeler, Angold, & Costello, 2007). Exposure to catastrophic events such as massive violence and natural disasters may present a different picture. Wang and his group (2006) looked at the differential impact of various types of trauma exposure on emotional and behavioral problems in preschool children in Israel and found a differential pattern of associations between the types of trauma exposure (direct exposure to terrorism, media exposure to terrorism, and other trauma) and children's internalizing and externalizing problems. They feel that this line of research is important for the identification of risk factors and the development of effective prevention and intervention strategies to promote resilience in preschool children. Another study from Israel looked at adolescent exposure to recurrent terrorism in a sample of 695 Israeli high school students. Using *DSM-IV* criteria, the prevalence of probable posttraumatic stress disorder was 7.6%. Girls reported greater severity of posttraumatic symptoms, whereas boys exhibited greater functional impairment in social and family domains. The authors note that school-based screening seems to be an effective means for identifying adolescents who have been exposed to terror and are experiencing posttraumatic stress symptomatology as well as psychosocial impairment (Pat-Horenczyk et al., 2007). In still another study from Israel, Finzi-Dottan and others (2006) looked at PTSD reactions among children with learning disabilities exposed to terror attacks and found that this was significantly higher than in a control group. Personal exposure to terror, past personal threatening life events, avoidant and anxious attachment, and the anxious attachment/threatening past events interaction contributed significantly to the explained variance of PTSD. The authors note that adolescents with learning disabilities seem to have trouble in cognitive processing of traumatic events.

John, Russell, and Russell (2007) looked at the prevalence of PTSD among children and adolescents after the tsunami disaster in southern India. This disaster, one of the largest disasters in recent history, resulted in the deaths of over 250,000 people and massive destruction in eight countries. Five hundred twenty-three juvenile survivors of the tsunami in southern India were studied to determine the prevalence of PTSD. Results of the study revealed a prevalence of 70.7% for acute PTSD and 10.9% for delayed onset PTSD. The condition was more prevalent among girls and more severe among adolescents exposed to loss of life or property. The authors note the importance of developing an effective, culturally sensitive outreach therapy for this group of survivors.

Diagnostic Instruments

Child Trauma Screening Questionnaire

A group of Australian investigators looked at the efficacy of using the Child Trauma Screening Questionnaire within two weeks of a traumatic accident which required hospitalization in 135 children to assess whether or not PTSD symptoms would be present one and six months later. This questionnaire correctly identified 82% of children who demonstrated distressing PTSD symptoms (9% of the sample) six months later and correctly screened out 74% of children who did not demonstrate such symptoms (Kenardy, Spence, & Macleod, 2006).

Prevention and Amelioration

Efforts After Hurricanes Katrina and Rita

After the displacement of students following hurricanes Katrina and Rita in 2005, schools in several states enrolled many young people from affected areas with potential mental health needs. Jaychox et al. (2007) studied the ways schools perceived the mental health needs of these students and what mental health programs they implemented. Mental health personnel at 29 public schools/school systems and 11 private or parochial schools in Louisiana, Alabama, Texas, and Mississippi were interviewed at two time points, spring and fall-winter of 2006. Schools tried diverse approaches to interventions, depending on preexisting mental health infrastructure and personnel, perceived needs of students, and barriers and facilitators in each system. The conclusions of the study showed that despite significant efforts to support affected students, schools were limited in their ability to implement disaster-focused programs. The authors feel that extension of crisis plans to include pre-crisis training in mental health programming for both students and staff who have ongoing difficulties after a disaster or crisis may be beneficial.

Exercise

Newman and Motta (2007) investigated the effects of aerobic exercise on childhood PTSD, depression, and anxiety in a group of fifteen participants residing in a residential treatment center. After an eight-week exercise program, consisting of 40 minutes of exercise three times per week, significant symptom improvement was documented.

CHAPTER 6

ANXIETY DISORDERS: OBSESSIVE-COMPULSIVE DISORDER

··

Diagnostic Criteria

Obsessive-compulsive disorder (OCD) is an anxiety disorder in which either obsessions or compulsions or both must be present. Obsessions are defined as recurrent and persistent thoughts, impulses, or images that are experienced, at some time during the disturbance, as intrusive and inappropriate and cause marked anxiety or distress. Thoughts, impulses, or images associated with obsessions are not simply excessive worries about real-life problems. The affected person tries to ignore or suppress these thoughts or images, or tries to neutralize them with some other thought or action. As an example, a person who is a "worrier" and who continually talks about problems they have with their children probably does not meet the criteria for OCD. A person with OCD recognizes that the obsessive thoughts, impulses, or images are a product of his or her own mind and are not the result of someone or something else causing them. Children and people who have ID may not understand this. As an example, an individual who has ID who feels that he must wash his hands until they bleed because he feels he is unclean would probably meet the criteria for OCD.

Compulsions

Compulsions are defined as repetitive behaviors such as hand washing, ordering, and checking or mental acts such as meditation or counting that the person feels driven to perform in response to an obsession. These typically "need" to be done according to strict rules that the person has established, consciously or unconsciously, for himself or herself. All of these rules or behaviors are aimed at preventing or reducing distress or preventing some dreaded event and at controlling the obsessions.

Types of Compulsions

There are various types of compulsions, one group of which is called completeness-incompleteness compulsions. These include a wide variety of things which finish or complete a task—even if the affected person has to re-do the task just to finish it. Examples for people with ID include insisting on closing open doors, taking all items out of a storage area, removing items and then returning them over and over, and insisting on doing a certain chore (not letting anyone else do it). These kinds of behavior in a person with ID would probably assist in making a diagnosis of OCD.

Cleaning-tidiness compulsions include opening a cupboard door and then closing it, over and over, touching or tapping an item repeatedly, going through a touching or stepping pattern, and unusual sniffing. Some people with autism spectrum disorders appear to go through some of these same rituals. Deviant grooming compulsions include picking at hand/face/legs etc. to the point of gouging skin, checking self in a mirror excessively, inappropriate hair cutting, and pulling out hair while sitting calmly.

Diagnostic Considerations

When working with people with ID, it is important to determine the number and types of compulsions and categories in which symptoms are present. Several checklists are available to assist in counting OCD symptoms—one is the Child Behavior Checklist (Gedye, 1996). Geller et al. (2006) found that the obsessive compulsive scale of the Child Behavior Checklist showed good reliability and validity and acceptable psychometric properties to help diagnose young people with OCD. Then, based on data, an assessment of the amount of interference with daily life should be made. One determination is to note if the compulsions take more than one hour/day if not prevented and if they significantly interfere with the person's daily return. Another determination to be made is a measurement of the response by the involved person when the compulsions are interrupted. Examples of these responses may include stopping momentarily, then resuming activity, waiting until the observer is gone, then resuming, becoming angry and aggressive toward the person who intervenes, biting or hitting self, and head-banging.

Increased diagnostic accuracy seems to result from utilizing clinician-rated scales containing information from both children and parents (Stewart, Ceranoglu, O'Hanley, & Geller, 2005).

Some cases of OCD as well as some cases of tic disorders seem to be the result of autoimmune responses to streptococcal infections (Dale, 2005; Dale, Hevman, Giovannoni, & Church, 2005; Hoekstra & Minderaa, 2005). Obsessive-compulsive disorders are more frequent in people with active or prior rheumatic fever (RF), which is a result of the body's response to a streptococcal infection (Hounie et al., 2007). Some sort of familial relationship seems to exist between OCD and RF, since if the person with RF also has OCD there is increased risk of OCD among first-degree relatives.

Childhood and Adolescent Issues

Apparently there are two peaks of age-of-onset for OCD—one peak in pre-adolescent childhood and the other peak in adulthood. Adult studies report equal gender representation or a slight female preponderance, but pediatric clinical samples are clearly male predominant. Patterns of psychiatric co-morbidity in both pediatric and adult OCD show high rates of tic and mood and anxiety disorders, but pediatric OCD is also distinctly associated with ADHD and oppositional defiant disorder as well as pervasive developmental disorders. Family studies indicate that OCD is highly familial and that a childhood onset seems to be associated with a markedly increased risk for familial transmission of OCD, tic disorders, and ADHD (Geller, 2006).

CHAPTER 7

CONDUCT DISORDER

....

Diagnostic Criteria

According to the *DSM-IV-TR*, the essential feature of conduct disorder is a repetitive and persistent pattern of behavior in which the basic rights of others or major age-appropriate norms and/or rules of society are violated. These behaviors fall into four major groupings: aggressive conduct that causes or threatens physical harm to other people or animals, non-aggressive conduct that causes property loss or damage, deceitfulness or theft, and serious violation of rules. Three or more behaviors must have been present during the past year, with at least one behavior present in the last six months. The behavior pattern is usually present in a variety of settings.

Intellectual Disability Issues

Obviously a great deal of difficulty is present when attempts are made to utilize standard criteria for persons with ID, particularly when the assumption is made in the general criteria that the person *understands* the basic rights of others and appropriate social behavior. There are numerous cases of people with ID showing aggression to people and/or animals and destroying property, but far fewer cases where deceitfulness or serious violation of rules is present—obviously the difference is the nature of the *intent* (Lee & Friedlander, 2007). One study in the United Kingdom looked at the contribution of socioeconomic position to the risk of various health and mental health problems in children with ID and found that 23% of the increased risk for conduct disorder seemed attributable to socioeconomic problems (Emerson & Hatton, 2007). Another study looked at misuse of various substances in people with ID in Ireland and found that alcohol was the main substance to be misused, with one-fifth of the substance users also using a combination of illicit drugs and/or prescribed medication (Taggart, McLaughlin, Quinn, & Milligan, 2006). About three-fourths of the sample were found to have been using alcohol for more than five years. Being male and young, having a borderline/mild level of ID, living independently, and having a mental health problem were found to be risk factors for developing a substance related problem. The authors feel that early identification may diminish the long-established patterns of use and associated behaviors. This early diagnosis is important for all young people with normal functioning, as well as those with ID, since adolescents with conduct disorder have a significantly increased risk of suicidal behavior if they have co-morbid alcohol dependence (Homaki, Rasanen, Viilo, & Haddo, 2007).

Childhood and Adolescence Issues

Onset

Onset of the disorder is either in childhood or adolescence. When the diagnosis is made in the childhood group the disorder is usually more serious than when the diagnosis is not made until adolescence (Hendren & Mullen, 2006). According to *DSM-IV-TR*, conduct disorder can't be diagnosed if the person is older than eighteen unless antisocial personality disorder is <u>not</u> present. Childhood-onset conduct disorder has been found to be associated with higher rates of attention-deficit hyperactivity disorder (ADHD) and anxiety disorders, male gender, and perceived and total hostility scores than conduct disorder beginning in adolescence (Connor, Ford, Albert, & Doerfler, 2007). Conduct disorder in childhood carries the highest risk of adult psychopathology of any mental health disorder present in childhood (Rutter, 2008).

Genetic and Environmental Factors

The role of genetic vulnerability ("nature") in the development of conduct disorder has not been fully worked out, but probably genetic factors play at least some part in the disorder, either directly or through a mediating factor such as temperament. Most studies looking at young people with disruptive behaviors suggest a significant role for psychosocial and environmental factors that, acting with genetic factors, significantly increase the risk of psychopathology (Hendren & Mullen, 2006). One study showed that chromosomes 2 and 19 may have regions conferring a risk for conduct disorder. Previous studies have noted that maternal smoking may be associated with conduct disorder in children. Monuteaux and his group (2006) feel that the association may be specific to overt, obvious symptoms of conduct disorder, rather than covert ("under-cover") symptoms. One study from Australia indicates that cruelty to animals may be an early manifestation of a subgroup of children developing conduct problems associated with traits of low empathy and callous disregard rather than externalizing problems and parenting problems (Dadds, Whiting, & Hawes, 2006).

Prevention and Amelioration

Some experts feel that one of the major pathways to delinquency and antisocial behavior in adolescence and later begins in the toddler years. Parents' failure to effectively punish aggressive behavior and teach reasonable levels of compliance may lead to an escalating spiral of coercive behavior among family members which trains a child to become progressively more antisocial (Brown, Kellam, Ialongo, Poduska, & Ford, 2007). Brotman and his group (2005b) investigated the immediate impact of an eight-month center-based and home-based prevention program for preschoolers at high risk for conduct problems. They felt their intervention yielded significant effects on negative parenting, parental encouragement for learning, and child social competence with peers. Brotman and another group (2005ba) also found that older siblings benefited from an intervention for at-risk preschoolers. Foster, Jones, and the Conduct Problems Prevention Research Group (2006) examined the cost-effectiveness of the Fast Track intervention, a multi-year, multi-component intervention designed to reduce violence among at-risk children. Initial examination of the total sample showed that the intervention was not cost-effective at likely levels of policymakers' willingness to pay for the key outcomes, but later analysis of those most at risk showed that the intervention likely was cost-effective given specified willingness-to-pay criteria. From a policy standpoint, the authors feel this finding is encouraging because such children are likely to generate higher costs for society over their lifetimes. Barriers to cost-effectiveness still remain, such as the ability to effectively identify and recruit such higher-risk children in future implementations. Reading (2007) looked at the cost-effectiveness of a parenting program for at-risk children and found that the program was carried out at a relatively low cost and was cost-effective compared with the waiting list control. The strong clinical effect appeared to suggest it would represent good value for money for public spending.

CHAPTER 8

ATTENTION-DEFICIT HYPERACTIVITY DISORDER

Diagnostic Criteria

According to the *DSM-IV-TR*, the essential feature of attention-deficit hyperactivity disorder (ADHD) is a persistent pattern of inattention and/or hyperactivity-impulsivity that is more frequently displayed and more severe than is typically observed in individuals at a comparable level of development. Some hyperactive-impulsive or inattentive symptoms that cause impairment must have been present before age seven, although many people are diagnosed when the symptoms have been present for a number of years, particularly those with only the inattentive symptoms. Some impairment from the symptoms must be present in at least two settings, and there must be clear evidence of interference with developmentally appropriate social, academic, or occupational functioning. The disturbance does not occur exclusively during the course of a pervasive developmental disorder, schizophrenia, or other psychotic disorder, and is not better accounted for by another disorder such as a mood disorder or personality disorder.

Childhood and Adolescence Issues

Inattention and Hyperactivity

Inattention may show up in academic, occupational, or social situations. People with this disorder may fail to pay close attention to details or may make careless mistakes in schoolwork or other tasks. Work is often messy, performed carelessly, and rarely given considered thought.

Hyperactivity may show up as squirming in one's seat, hopping up and down, climbing at inappropriate times, and other, similar behavior. In children with ID, symptoms are more apt to show up in group settings. Neither language ability nor the ability to report emotions is required to make the diagnosis in this group (Lee & Friedlander, 2007).

ADHD and ID

Almost all the studies applying *DSM-IV* diagnostic criteria for ADHD in people with ID have been done in children in the 6-to-11 age group. No studies have been reported in this population using ICD-10 criteria. Lee and Friedlander (2007) point out that most research studies include an over-reliance on parent and teacher rating scales, which they feel tend to over-diagnose ADHD, and that some studies include a wide-range of I.Q. levels.

Increased Vulnerability to Acccidents

Brook and Boaz (2006) studied a group of 108 high school students with both ADHD and learning disabilities and found a real risk for these adolescents to be involved in all kinds of accidents in a variety of settings. Methods for accident prevention should be particularly outlined to these students and their families.

Thorough Assessment and Differential Diagnosis

Waslick and Greenhall (2006) note that even though oppositional defiant disorder and conduct disorder are highly associated with ADHD, the distinction between these three disorders is supported by empirical evidence. They point out the importance of synthesizing information obtained from multiple sources, since the information obtained from adults and from the individual child are often quite different. Children with ADHD should receive a complete medical evaluation, since occasionally a standard physical examination may reveal neurologic problems that completely explain the child's inattentiveness, restlessness, and impulsivity—such as the fact that children with partial deafness or very poor vision may appear inattentive and restless to the teacher. A child who has an itchy skin rash or pinworms may be so uncomfortable that he or she is restless and disruptive.

Genetic and Environmental Factors

The precise cause of ADHD is unknown. It is often a familial disorder and is likely to have a genetic component ("nature" factor). Children of adults with a history of childhood-onset ADHD are at high risk for developing the disorder—four times the risk of those in the general population (Glatt, Faraone, & Tsuang, 2007). Maternal smoking during pregnancy seems to be a risk factor for development of ADHD in the child. Infants with low birth weight and evidence of white matter brain injury may also be at increased risk.

Some studies have shown that there may be some genetic influences that affect ADHD and autism spectrum disorders—some sets of genes may increase the risk for both disorders. According to Reiersen and her group (2008), the form of ADHD that has the strongest association with autism spectrum disorders is a disorder characterized by a high degree of both inattentive and hyperactive symptoms.

Persistence of Symptoms

Several studies suggest that some symptoms of ADHD—particularly hyperactivity—tend towards remission over time, but inattention problems are very persistent (Waslick & Greenhill, 2006). Some studies suggest that there may be different outcomes for the different core symptoms—inattention symptoms tend to predict problems with educational achievement, but prominent hyperactivity and impulsivity symptoms may lead to greater risk of antisocial outcomes.

CHAPTER 9

SCHIZOPHRENIA & OTHER PSYCHOTIC DISORDERS

Diagnostic Criteria

The diagnosis of schizophrenia in children and adolescents as well as in adults is currently made by using the *DSM-IV-TR* criteria. The active phase of the disorder is marked by at least two of the following symptoms, each present for a significant portion of time during a one-month period: delusions, hallucinations, disorganized speech, grossly disorganized or catatonic behavior, and negative symptoms such as flat affect, alogia (inability to speak), and avolition (lack of movement) (Tsai & Champine, 2006). In addition to these symptoms, there must also be a marked deterioration in social or occupational functioning, present for a significant amount of time since the onset of the disturbance, but for child/adolescent schizophrenia the criterion is modified to "failure to achieve expected level of interpersonal, academic, or occupational achievement." In making a diagnosis, mood disorders and schizoaffective disorders must be ruled. Since adolescents with bipolar disorder often present with manic episodes that look like psychosis, the distinction between disorders in this age group is particularly important.

As noted earlier, schizophrenia is difficult to diagnosis accurately in persons with ID, largely because of communication problems. Actual incidence in this population has not been determined.

Childhood and Adolescence Issues

Hallucinations

Schizophrenia seldom becomes apparent in children before age nine. The onset of the disorder in children is usually insidious—acute onset is relatively rare. Askenazy and his group (2007) looked at auditory hallucination in pre-pubertal children in an attempt to establish links with various *DSM-IV* diagnoses and to look at the development of hallucinations over a 12-month period. In a group of 90 children, 16 reported auditory hallucinations. In 53%, they observed full recovery from hallucinations within three months, and all of these had anxiety disorders. In 30%, hallucinations persisted over 12 months, and all showed conduct disorders at this point in time. None were diagnosed as having schizophrenia, but this study was published very recently, and long-term outcomes are not yet available.

Genetic Risk

The 22q11.2 deletion syndrome is the most common known genetic risk factor for the development of schizophrenia. Gothelf et al. (2007) conducted a longitudinal study of 60 adolescents with this syndrome as compared to 29 children matched for age and I.Q., beginning between 1998 and followed up between 2003 and 2005. The two groups had similar baseline neuropsychiatric profiles. At follow-up, 32.1% of those with the deletion syndrome had developed psychotic disorders as compared with 4.3% of those without. Lower baseline verbal I.Q. was also associated with more severe psychotic symptoms at follow-up evaluation. The authors concluded that early intervention in the subgroup of children with sub-threshold signs of psychosis and internalizing symptoms, especially anxiety symptoms, may reduce the risk of developing psychotic disorders during adolescence. Children with the 22q11.2 deletion also have a high rate of autistic disorders (Vorstman et al., 2006).

Prevention and Amelioration

Fostering Social Relationships

Social contexts, particularly neighborhoods in which people live, seem to have significant impact on the incidence of schizophrenia. When looking at the incidence in immigrant populations, the incidence of psychotic disorders for people who are foreign born are significantly lower in areas primarily populated by their own members. Even if neighborhoods cannot be chosen in this way, significant relationships can be fostered between people of the same national background, which should also help prevent psychotic problems (March & Dana, 2008).

Early Intervention

Several groups have studied the impact of early diagnosis or at least recognition of the possibility of early-onset schizophrenia and have found that working with families seems to be beneficial both in slowing the course of the disease and preventing some of the more serious life-time problems (Collins, 2002; Kumra, Nicholson, & Rapoport, 2002). When early intervention is used when symptoms are beginning to develop and the individual appears to be having an incipient first-episode psychosis, long-term outcome is improved, response to treatment is better, and there is a greater likelihood of remission (Bassett, Chow, & Hodgkinson, 2008).

CHAPTER 10

AUTISM SPECTRUM DISORDERS

Prevalence

Two to five of every 10,000 individuals have autistic disorder, but as many as 23 of every 10,000 people have conditions that may fall within the autistic-pervasive developmental disorder spectrum. The actual incidence of autism spectrum disorders is really unknown, but the incidence is probably not increasing, since diagnostic criteria have been greatly widened in recent years.

Diagnostic Criteria

Diagnostic criteria include impairment in social interaction, impairment in communication, and restricted repetitive and stereotyped patterns of behavior, interests, and activities (American Psychiatric Association, 2000).

Childhood and Adolescence Issues and Diagnostic Instruments

Early Identification

Early identification and intensive intervention during early childhood result in improved outcomes for most children with pervasive developmental disorders (PDDs) (Jellinek et al., 2002a). Cox and his group (1999) studied the association between, and stability of, clinical diagnosis and diagnosis derived from the Autism Diagnostic Interview-Revised (ADI-R) in a sample of prospectively identified children with childhood autism and other pervasive developmental disorders assessed at the ages of 20 months and 42 months. Clinical diagnosis of autism was stable, with all children diagnosed at 20 months receiving a diagnosis of autism or PDD at 42 months. Clinical diagnosis for PDD and Asperger syndrome lacked sensitivity at 20 months, with several children who subsequently received these diagnoses at 42 months receiving diagnoses of language disorder or general developmental delay at first assessment. Two later-diagnosed children were considered clinically normal at the early time point. The ADI-R was found to have good specificity but poor sensitivity at detecting autism at 20 months, but the stability of diagnosis from 20 to 42 months was good. The ADI-R at age 20 months was not sensitive to the detection of related PDDs or Asperger syndrome.

Ethnicity and Diagnosis

Differences by ethnicity in the diagnoses assigned prior to the diagnosis of autism were evaluated by Mandell, Ittenbach, Levy, and Pinto-Martin (2007). They examined charts of 406 Medicaid-eligible children, and in this sample African Americans were 2.6 times less likely than white children to receive an autism diagnosis on their first specialty care visit. Among children who did not receive an autism diagnosis on their first visit, ADHD was the most common diagnosis. African-American children were 5.1 times more likely than white children to receive a diagnosis of adjustment disorder than of ADHD and 2.4 times more likely to receive a diagnosis of conduct disorder than of ADHD. Differences in these diagnostic patterns by ethnicity suggest to the authors of this study possible variations in parents' descriptions of symptoms, clinician interpretations and expectations, or symptom presentation.

Covariant Psychiatric Disorders

Prevalence of Comorbid Disorders

Many clinicians and investigators have found that in addition to the core symptoms of autism spectrum disorders, a great number of people on this spectrum develop other behavioral and/or psychiatric symptoms that may be looked at as clinical manifestations of co-morbid psychiatric disorders, although investigators have not yet specifically examined the actual incidence of these disorders. One review of various studies found wide ranges of estimates of incidence, such as 17-74% of individuals with autism spectrum disorders have anxiety and/or fears and 9-44% show depressive mood, irritability, agitation, and inappropriate affect (Tsai, 2006). The *DSM-IV-TR* makes very little mention of co-occurring mental health conditions but does note that that those with autism with "intellectual capacity for insight" may become depressed when they realize their severe impairment (American Psychiatric Association, 2000, p. 72). The *DSM-IV-TR* also mentions that an additional diagnosis of schizophrenia may be made if persistent delusions or hallucinations develop in a person with autism (p. 74). In the *DM-ID*, Bonfardin, Zimmerman, and Gaus (2007) note that persons with Asperger disorder or high-functioning autism may present in a mental health setting with apparent psychiatric symptoms before their Asperger disorder is recognized, since that diagnosis was not formally made available until 1994.

Historically, Michelangelo may have met present day criteria for Asperger disorder and also had depression, among other health problems (Fitzgerald, 2004).

Gillberg and Billstedt (2000) selectively reviewed the literature detailing data pertaining to symptoms and disorders associated with autism or Asperger disorder and found descriptions of a large number of medical conditions, psychiatric disorders, and behavioral and motor dyscontrol syndromes. They recommended that studies of large general population samples where co-morbidity patterns can be analyzed without bias should receive high priority.

Ghaziuddin, Weidmer-Mikhail, and Ghaziuddin (1998) studied a group of 35 individuals with Asperger disorder for additional psychiatric disorders at the time of initial evaluation and during a two-year follow-up and found that 23 (65%) had psychiatric symptoms.

Underlying Genetic Factors

Duvall et al. (2007), noting that autism is a complex genetic disorder with a highly mixed phenotype, did a genome-wide scan for a social endophenotype in autism using the Social Responsiveness

Scale, primarily looking at social relatedness in the whole family. They feel that their study shows the utility of this scale to detect autism-related genetic loci that may more closely relate to underlying genetic factors.

Autism Spectrum Disorders and Intellectual Disability

While very little has been published in the scientific literature about the incidence of mental health conditions in persons with autism spectrum disorders, a few case reports have been described. When the topic has been discussed, it usually has been in the context of those with coexisting intellectual disability, and not usually with high-functioning autism or Asperger disorder, although interest in these groups has increased lately (Matson & Nebel-Schwalm, 2006). Bradley and colleagues (2004) compared a group of 12 adolescents and young adults with severe ID and autism with 12 who had severe ID without autism, and found that those with autism showed significantly greater disturbances as measured by the Diagnostic Assessment for the Severely Handicapped-II test.

Tsakanidos and colleagues (2006) examined psychiatric comorbidity in 147 adults with ID and autism and 605 adults with ID without autism and found that the individuals with both ID and autism were no more likely to receive a psychiatric diagnosis than people with ID only. People with autism were significantly less likely to receive a diagnosis of personality disorder.

Gender Differences and Coexisting Psychopathology

Holtmann, Bolte, and Poustka (2007) looked at gender differences in individuals with autism and coexisting psychopathology and found that females had more trouble than males with severe social and attention problems. They suggest that further research should compare the cognitive phenotype of autism between genders.

Case Reports

Various other case reports of interest have been becoming available for some time. Cook, Kefir, Charak, and Leventhal (1993) described an adolescent boy with autistic disorder who had a history of being physically abused who met *DSM-III-R* criteria for post-traumatic stress disorder. In 2004, Fontenelle and colleagues described a man with Asperger syndrome, obsessive-compulsive disorder, and major depression who had a 45,X/46,XY chromosomal mosaicism. Bolte and Bosch (2005) reported the long-term outcome in two women with autism spectrum disorder, diagnosed in childhood by Bosch, one of whom developed anxiety disorder and the other schizoaffective symptoms. They continue to manifest definite autistic traits.

In 2005, Yamasue and his group described the neuroanatomy of monozygotic twins with Asperger disorder, only one of whom had depression. Naidu, James, Mukatoeva-Ladinska, and Briel (2006) reported the diagnosis of Asperger syndrome in a 66-year-old man presenting with depression. Apparently the depression was diagnosed before the Asperger disorder. Nylander and Gillberg in 2001 recommended that a brief screening questionnaire, the Autism Spectrum Disorder in Adults Screening Questionnaire, be used in adults with psychiatric disorders when some symptoms of autism seem to be present.

Autism and OCD: Differences in Repetitive Thoughts and Behaviors

McDougle et al. (1995) investigated the types of repetitive thoughts and behavior demonstrated by adults with autistic disorder compared to a group of age- and gender-matched adults with obsessive-compulsive disorder (OCD) and found that the repetitive thoughts and behavior characteristics of autism differed significantly from the symptoms of those with OCD. The group with autism was significantly less likely to experience cleaning, checking, and counting behavior, but more likely to have hoarding, telling or asking, touching, tapping, rubbing, and self-damaging/self-mutilating behavior.

Intact Brain Function

Bernier, Dawson, Panagiotides, and Webb (2005) studied 14 adolescents and adults diagnosed with autism spectrum disorder and 14 typical individuals matched for age, gender, I.Q., and anxiety level. The researchers utilized a fear potentiated startle paradigm to examine brain amygdala function and found no significant difference between the groups. They concluded that this aspect of amygdala function seemed to be intact in the individuals with autism.

Autism and Depression

Depressive disorders have been of concern to several researchers. Berthoz and Hill (2005) examined the validity of using self-report to assess emotion regulation abilities in 27 adults with autism spectrum disorders and 35 adults without autism spectrum disorders. They found that individuals with autism spectrum disorders appeared more depressed and less able to regulate emotion than controls, with increased difficulties in the cognitive domain rather than in the affective aspects. Stewart, Barnard, Pearson, Hasan, and O'Brien (2006) speculated that depression is common in autism spectrum disorders, but they noted very little research, probably because of diagnostic difficulties and the overlap of symptoms in autism and depression, such as social withdrawal and appetite and sleep disturbance. Impaired verbal and non-verbal communication can mask the symptoms of depression, but symptoms associated with autism and Asperger syndrome such as obsessionality and self-injury may be increased during an episode of depression. Ghaziuddin and colleagues (2002) noted that emerging evidence indicates that depression is probably the most common psychiatric disorder that occurs in persons with autism.

Matson and Nebel-Schwalm (2006) noted the meager research findings on depression and autism spectrum disorders and described the complex assessment issues involved. According to these authors, identifying comorbidity of depression is more than an academic exercise because depression can negatively impact long term outcome, significantly increasing the individual's risk for suicide, greater levels of withdrawal, noncompliance, and aggression.

Autism and Sleep Disturbances

Liu, Hubbard, Fabes, and Adam (2006) looked at sleep disturbances of children with autism spectrum disorders and found that both dyssomnias and parasomnias are very prevalent in children with these disorders. They feel that although multiple child and family factors are associated with sleep problems, other comorbid disorders may play a major role.

Autism and Schizophrenia

While in the past experts believed that autism and schizophrenia were related, considerable evidence in the last several decades suggests that this is not true. Volkmar and Cohen (1991) examined detailed case records of 163 adolescents and adults with well-documented histories of autism and found only one person with an unequivocal history of schizophrenia, which is roughly comparable to the frequency of schizophrenia in the general population.

Screening Children with ASD for Related Psychiatric Conditions

Matson and his colleagues at Louisiana State University are presently field testing an instrument for screening children with autism spectrum disorders for related psychiatric conditions (J. Matson, personal communication, April 19, 2007). Hopefully this will be useful for individuals of all ages.

Prevention and Amelioration

Training Course for Parents

McConachie, Randle, Hammal, and LeCouteur (2005) evaluated a training course for parents designed to help them understand autism spectrum disorders and to facilitate social communication with their young child. Parents received either immediate intervention or delayed access to the course. Fifty-one children aged 24 to 48 months were involved. Outcome was measured seven months after beginning of the study in parents' use of facilitative strategies, stress adaptation to the child, children's vocabulary size, behavior problems, and social skills. The training course was well received by parents and had a measurable effect on both parents' and children's communication skills.

Early Interventions

While the nature-nurture components of autistic spectrum disorders are complex, the risk of an individual developing autism if he/she has an affected sibling is illustrated quite clearly from family study data—they have about a 22-fold increased risk (Glatt et al., 2007; Solomon, Hessl, Chiu, Hagerman, & Hendren, 2007). Thus siblings of children with autism are, or should be, prime targets for the development and validation of effective early interventions, since recent (Evans, 2006) evidence suggests that a small minority of children with an autism spectrum disorder can recover from the condition to near-normal levels with only mild residual deficits when treated with applied behavior analysis. Final results from a number of studies in this area are not yet in. In a less scientific, but quite effective management program for any child, the Academy of Pediatrics has published a manual for all parents, *A Parent's Guide to Building Resilience in Children and Teens: Giving Your Child Roots and Wings* (Ginsburg, 2006), which should be quite helpful for parents of children with autism spectrum disorders as well as others.

CHAPTER 11

CONCLUSIONS

We have come a long way in understanding and serving young people with mental health/behavioral disorders in the past fifty years. For example, most of us do not continue to blame mothers for the autistic disorder in their children (Grinker, 2007). Tools for screening children for a number of behavioral patterns are now available and can be utilized in a variety of settings. When screening is positive, various methods to help families and others work with these children are now showing positive results in the lives of children and young people.

Exciting discoveries in the field of genetics are being made and reported every day, but the more that is learned in genetics the more complex the whole field has become. There seems to be no simple genetic pattern that will easily facilitate diagnosis. Two new texts that discuss these complexities in detail have just come out (Hudziak, 2008; Smoller, Sheidley, & Tsuang, 2008). The lay press often reports new developments in genetics (and in other health areas) in a simplistic manner that leads people to think that all the final answers to complex conditions are being discovered. Fortunately, some developments are being reported more accurately (Hotz, 2008), which is an encouraging sign.

When we consider where we should go from here, we need to carefully assess all new findings in genetics, but we also need to remember that all psychiatric conditions seem to due to both genetic issues and "nurture" issues, so we also need to continue to seek ways to make environments more conducive to children and young people developing resilience. We need to assess reports of all sorts about this and look for ways to adjust techniques that are successful in one environment to increase success in other environments, including in families, schools, and other community settings.

LIST OF ABBREVIATIONS

ADHD	Attention-Deficit/Hyperactivity Disorder
ADI-R	Autism Diagnostic Interview-Revised
ASD	Autism Spectrum Disorder
CBCL	Child Behavior Checklist
CCB	Checklist of Challenging Behavior
CDI	Children's Depression Inventory
CDC	Centers for Disease Control and Prevention
DCR	Diagnostic Criteria for Research
DM-ID	*Diagnostic Manual –Intellectual Disability: A Textbook of Diagnosis of Mental Disorders in Persons with Intellectual Disability*
DSM	*Diagnostic and Statistical Manual of Mental Disorders*
DST	Dexamethasine Suppression Test
ID	Intellectual Disability
IQ	Intelligence Quotient
NADD	National Association for the Dually Diagnosed
NIMH	National Institute for Mental Health
OCD	Obsessive-Compulsive Disorder
PASS –ADD	Psychiatric Assessment Schedule for Adults with Developmental Disability
PDD	Pervasive Developmental Disorder
PIRMA	Psychopathology Instrument for Mentally Retarded Adults
PTSD	Posttraumatic Stress Disorder
RF	Rheumatic Fever
SRDQ	Self-Report Depression Questionnaire

REFERENCES

Ailey, S. H. (2000). Screening adolescents with mental retardation for depression. *Journal of School Nursing, 16*, 6-11.

Alfanto, C. A., Ginsburg, G. S., & Kingery, J. N. (2007). Sleep-related problems among children and adolescents with anxiety disorders. *Journal of the American Academy of Child & Adolescent Psychiatry, 46*, 224-232.

American Psychiatric Association (1987). *Diagnostic and statistical manual of mental disorders (3rd ed., revised)*. Washington, DC: Author.

American Psychiatric Association. (2000). *Diagnostic and Statistical Manual of Mental Disorders (4th ed., text revision, DSM-IV-TR)*. Washington, DC: Author.

Askenazy, F. L., Lestideau, K., Mevnadier, A., Dor, E., Mvquel, M., & Lecrubier, Y. (2007). Auditory hallucinations in pre-pubertal children: a one-year follow-up, preliminary findings. *European Child & Adolescent Psychiatry, 16*, 411-415.

Attari, A., Dashty, S., & Mahmoodi, M. (2006). Post-traumatic stress disorder in children witnessing a public hanging in the Islamic Republic of Iran. *Eastern Mediterranean Health Journal, 12*, 72-80.

Balboni, G., Battagliese, G., & Pedrabissi, L. (2000). The Psychopathology Inventory for Mentally Retarded Adults: Factor structure and comparisons between subjects with or without dual diagnosis. *Research in Developmental Disabilities, 21*, 311-321.

Bassett, A. S., chow, E. W. C., & Hodgkinson, K. A. (2008). Genetics of schizophrenia and psychotic disorders. In J. W. Smoller, B. R. Sheidley, & M. T. Tsuang (Eds.), *Psychiatric genetics: Applications in clinical practice* (pp. 99-130). Arlington, VA: American Psychiatric Publishing, Inc.

Beardslee, W. R., Gladstone, T. R., Wright, E. J., & Cooper, A. B. (2003). A family-based approach to the prevention of depressive symptoms in children at Risk: Evidence of parental and child change. *Pediatrics, 112*, 119-131.

Benavidez, D. A., & Matson, J. L. (1993). Assessment of depression in mentally retarded adolescents. *Research in Developmental Disabilities, 14,* 179-188.

Benson, B. A., Reiss, S., Smith, D. C., & Laman, D. S. (1985). Psychosocial correlates of depression in mentally retarded adults. II: Poor social skills. *American Journal on Mental Deficiency, 89,* 657-659.

Berman, M. E. (1967). Mental retardation and depression. *Mental Retardation, 5 (6),* 19-21.

Bernier, R., Dawson, G., Panagiotides, H., & Webb, S. (2005). Individuals with autism spectrum disorder show normal responses to a fear potential startle paradigm. *Journal of Autism & Developmental Disorder, 35,* 575-583.

Berthoz, S., & Hill, E. L. (2005). The validity of using self-reports to assess emotion regulation abilities in adults with autism spectrum disorder. *European Psychiatry, 20,* 291-298.

Biederman, J., Petty, C., Faraone, S. V., Henin, A., Hirshfield-Becker, D., Pollack, M. H. et al. (2006). Effects of parental anxiety disorders in children at high risk for panic disorder: A controlled study. *Journal of Affective Disorders, 94,* 191-197.

Bolte, S., & Bosch, G. (2005). The long-term outcome in two females with autism spectrum disorder. *Psychopathology, 38,* 151-154.

Bonfardin, B., Zimmerman, A. W., & Gaus, V. (2007). Pervasive developmental disorders. In R. Fletcher, E. Loschen, Stavrakaki, C., & First, M. (Eds.), *Diagnostic manual—intellectual disability: A textbook of Diagnosis of mental disorders in persons with intellectual disability* (pp. 107-125). Kingston, NY: NADD Press.

Boyce, C. A., Heinssen, R., Ferrell, C. B., & Nakamura, R. K. (2007). Prospects for the prevention of mental illness. In M. T. Tsuang, W. S. Stone, & M. J. Lyons (Eds.), *Recognition and prevention of major mental and substance use disorders* (pp. 241-261). Washington, DC: American Psychiatric Press.

Bradley, E. A., Summers, J. A., Wood, H. L., & Bryson, S. E. (2004). Comparing rates of psychiatric and behavior disorders in adolescents and young adults with severe intellectual disability with and without autism. *Journal of Autism & Developmental Disorders, 34,* 151-161.

Breslau, N., Lucia, V. C., & Alvarado, G. F. (2006). Intelligence and other predisposing factors in exposure to trauma and post-traumatic stress disorder: A follow-up study at age 17 years. *Archives of General Psychiatry, 63*, 1238-1245.

Brook, U. & Boaz, M. (2006). Adolescents with attention deficit and hyperactivity disorder/learning disability and their prone-ness to accidents. *Indian Journal of Pediatrics, 73*, 299-303.

Brotman, L. M., Dawson-McClure, S., Gouley, K. K., McGuire, K., Burraston, B., & Bank, L. (2005a). Older siblings benefit from a family-based preventive intervention for preschoolers at risk for conduct problems. *Journal of Family Psychology, 19*, 581-591.

Brotman, L. M., Gouley, K. K., Chesir-Teran, D., Dennis, T., Klein, R. G., & Shrout, P. (2005b). Prevention for preschoolers at high risk for conduct problems: Immediate outcomes on parenting practices and child social competence. *Journal of Clinical Child & adolescent Psychology, 34*, 724-734.

Brown, C. H., Kellam, S. G., Ialongo, N., Poduska, J., & Ford, C. (2007). Prevention of aggressive behavior through middle school using a first-grade classroom-based intervention. In M. T. Tsuang, W. S. Stone, & M. J. Lyons (Eds.), *Recognition and prevention of major mental and substance use disorders* (pp. 347-369). Washington, DC: American Psychiatric Publishing, Inc.

Bryant, R. A., Salmon, K., Sinclair, E., & Davidson, P. (2007). Heart rate as a predictor of posttraumatic stress disorder in children. *General Hospital Psychiatry, 29*, 66-68.

Carter, A. S., Briggs-Gowan, M. J., & Davis, N. O. (2004). Assessment of young children's social-emotional development and psycho-pathology: Recent advances and recommendations for practice. *Journal of Child Psychology and Psychiatry, 45*, 109-134.

Carvill, S. (2001). Sensory impairments, intellectual disability, and psychiatry. *Journal of Intellectual Disability Research, 45*, 467-483.

Centers for Disease Control & Prevention. (2005a). The role of public health in mental health promotion. *Morbidity & Mortality Weekly Report, 54*, 841-842.

Centers for Disease Control & Prevention. (2005b). Mental health in the United States: Health care and well being of children with chronic emotional, behavioral, or developmental problems—United States, 2001. *Morbidity & Mortality Weekly Report, 54*, 985-989.

Chang, K., Howe, M., Gallelli, K., & Miklowitz, D. (2006). Prevention of pediatric bipolar disorder: Integration of neurobiological and psychosocial processes. *Annals of the New York Academy of Science, 1094*, 235-247.

Charlot, L. R., Doucette, A. C., & Mezzacappa, E. (1993). Affective symptoms of institutionalized adults with mental retardation. *American Journal on Mental Retardation, 85*, 408-416.

Charlot, L., Fox, S., Silka, V. R., Hurley, A., Lowry, M. A., & Pary, R. (2007). Mood disorders. In R. Fletcher, E. Loschen, Stavrakaki, C., & First, M. (Eds.), *Diagnostic manual—intellectual disability: A textbook of Diagnosis of mental disorders in persons with intellectual disability* (pp. 271-316). Kingston, NY: NADD Press.

Clarke, D. J., & Gomez, G. A. (1999). Utility of modified DCR-10 criteria in the diagnosis of depression associated with intellectual disability. *Journal of Intellectual Disability Research, 43*, 413-420.

Clinical capsules: Apnea common in epilepsy. (2003, April 15). *Family Practice News*, p. 35.

Collins, A. A. (2002). Family intervention in the early stage of schizophrenia. In R. B. Zipursky & S. C. Schulz (Eds.), *The early stages of schizophrenia* (pp. 129-156. Washington, DC: American Psychiatric Publishing, Inc..

Connor, D. E., Ford, J. D., Albert, D. B., & Doerfler, L. A. (2007). Conduct disorder subtype and comorbidity. *Annals of Clinical Psychiatry, 19*, 161-168.

Cook, E. H., Kefir, J. E., Charak, D. A., & Leventhal, B. L. (1993). Autistic disorder and post-traumatic stress disorder. *Journal of the American Academy of Child & Adolescent Psychiatry, 32*, 1292-1294.

Cooke, L. B., & Thompson, C. (1998). Seasonal Affective Disorder and response to light in two patients with learning disability. *Journal of Affective Disorders, 48*, 145-148.

Cooper, S. A. (1997). Epidemiology of psychiatric disorders in elderly compared with younger adults with learning disabilities. *British Journal of Psychiatry, 170*, 375-380.

Copeland, W. E., Keeler, G., Angold, A., & Costello, E. J. (2007). Traumatic events and posttraumatic stress in childhood. *Archives of General Psychiatry, 64*, 577-584.

Cox, A., Klein, K., Charman, T., Baird, G., Baron-Cohen, S., Swettenham, J., et al. (1999). Autism spectrum disorders at 20 and 42 months of age: Stability of clinical and ADI-R diagnosis. *Journal of Child Psychology & Psychiatry, 40*, 719-732.

Cutuli, J. J., Chaplin, T. M., Gillham, J. E., Reivich, K. J., & Seligman, M. A. (2006). Preventing co-occurring depression symptoms in adolescents with conduct problems. *Annals of the N.Y. Academy of Science, 1094*, 232-286.

Dadds, M. R., Whiting, C., & Hawes, D. J. (2006). Associations among cruelty to animals, family conflict, and psychopathic traits in childhood. *Journal of Interpersonal Violence, 21*, 411-429.

Dagnan, D., & Sandhu, S. (1999). Social comparison, self-esteem, and depression in people with intellectual disability. *Journal of Intellectual Disability Research, 43*, 372-379.

Dale, R. C. (2005). Post-streptococcal autoimmune disorders of the central nervous system. *Developmental Medicine & Child Neurology, 47*, 785-791.

Dale, R. C., Hevman, I., Giovannoni, G., & Church, A. W. (2005). Incidence of anti-brain antibodies in children with obsessive-compulsive disorder. *British Journal of Psychiatry, 187*, 314-319.

Davis, J. P., Judd, F. K., & Herrman, H. (1997). Depression in adults with intellectual disability. Part 1: A review. *Australian & New Zealand Journal of Psychiatry, 31*, 232-242.

Deb, S., Matthews, T., Holt, G., & Bouras, N. (2001). *Practice guidelines for the assessment and diagnosis of mental health problems in adults with intellectual disability* (pp. 47-56). Brighton, UK: Pavilion.

Deb, S., Thomas, M., & Bright, C. (2001). Mental disorder in adults with intellectual disability. I: Prevalence of functional psychiatric illness among a community based population aged between 16 and 24 years. *Journal of Intellectual Disability Research, 45*, 495-505.

Dubovsky, S. L., Davies, R., & Dubovsky, A. N. (2003). Mood disorders. In R. E. Hales & S. C. Yudofsky (Eds.), *Textbook of Clinical Psychiatry* (4th ed.), (pp. 439-542). Washington, DC: American Psychiatric Publishing, Inc.

Duvall, J. A., Lu, A., Cantor, R. M., Todd, R. D., Constantino, J. N., & Geschwind, D. H. (2007). A quantitative trait locus analysis of social responsiveness in multiplex autism families. *American Journal of Psychiatry, 164*, 656-662.

Emerson, E. & Hatton, C. (2007). Contribution of socioeconomic position to health inequalities of British children and adolescents with intellectual disability. *American Journal on Mental Retardation, 112*, 140-150.

Evans, J. (2006, May 15). Some do recover from autistic spectrum disorder. *Family Practice News*, p. 41.

Faust, D. S., Walker, D., & Sands, M. (2006). Diagnosis and management of childhood bipolar disorder in the primary care setting. *Clinical Pediatrics, 45*, 801-808.

Finzi-Dottan, R., Dekel, R., Lavi, T., & Su'ali, T. (2006). Post-traumaatic stress disorder reactions among children with learning disabilities exposed to terror attacks. *Comprehensive Psychiatry, 47*, 144-151.

Fitzgerald, A. M. (2004). Did Michelangelo (1475-1564) have high-functioning autism?. *Journal of Medical Biography, 12*, 126-127.

Fletcher, R., Loschen, E., Stavrakaki, C., & First, M. (Eds.), 2007. *Diagnostic manual-intellectual disability* (DM-ID). Kingston, NY: NADD Press.

Fitzgerald, A. M. (2004). Did Michelangelo (1475-1564) have high-functioning autism?. *Journal of Medical Biography, 12*, 126-127.

Foster, E. M., Jones, D., & Conduct Problems Prevention Research Group. (2006). Can a costly intervention be cost-effective?: An analysis of violence prevention. *Archives of General Psychiatry, 63*, 1284-1291.

Ganz, M. L. & Tendulkar, S. A. (2006). Mental health care services for children with special health care needs and their family members: Prevalence and correlates of unmet needs. *Pediatrics, 117*, 2138-2148.

Garber, J. (2006). Depression in children and adolescents: Linking risk research and prevention. *American Journal of Preventive Medicine, 31 (6 Suppl. 1)*, S104-125.

Gardner, W. I. (1967). Occurrence of severe depressive reactions in the mentally retarded. *American Journal of Psychiatry, 124*, 142-144.

Gedye, A. (1996). Issues involved in recognizing Obsessive-Compulsive Disorder in developmentally disabled clients. *Seminars in Clinical Neuropsychiatry, 1*, 142-147.

Geller, B., Tillman, R., & Bolhofner, K. (2007). Proposed definitions of bipolar I disorder episodes and daily rapid cycling phenomena in preschoolers, school-aged children, adolescents, and adults. *Journal of Child & Adolescent Psychopharmacology, 17*, 217-222.

Geller, D. A. (2006). Obsessive-compulsive and spectrum disorders in children and adolescents. *Psychiatric Clinics of North America, 29*, 353-370.

Geller, D. A., Doyle, R., Shaw, D., Mullin, B., Coffey, B., Petty, C., et al. (2006). A quick and reliable screening measure for OCD in youth: Reliability and validity of the obsessive compulsive scale of the Child Behavior Checklist. *Comprehensive Psychiatry, 47*, 234-240.

Gewirtz, A. H.. (2007). Promoting children's mental health in family supportive housing: A community-university partnership for formerly homeless children and families. *Journal of Primary Prevention, 28*, 359-374.

Ghaziuddin, M., Alessi, N., & Greden, J. F. (1995). Life events and depression in children with pervasive developmental disorders. *Journal of Autism & Developmental Disorders, 25*, 495-502.

Ghaziuddin, M., Ghaziuddin, N., & Greden, J. (2002). Depression in persons with autism: Implications for research and clinical care. *Journal of autism & Developmental Disorders, 32,* 299-306.

Ghaziuddin, M., Weidmer-Mikhail, E., & Ghazziuddin, N. (1998). Comorbidity of Asperger syndrome: A preliminary report. *Journal of Intellectual Disability Research, 42,* 279-283.

Gilberg, C., & Billstedt, E. (2000). Autism and Asperger syndrome: Coexistence with other clinical disorders. *Acta Psychiatrica Scandinavika, 102,* 321-330.

Ginsburg, K. R. (2006). *A parent's guide to building resilience in children and teens: Giving your child roots and wings.* Chicago, IL: American Academy of Pediatrics.

Glatt, S. J., Faraone, S. V., & Tsuang, M. T. (2007). Genetic risk factors for mental disorders: General principles and state of the science. In M. T. Tsuang, W. S. Stone, & M. J. Lyones (Eds.), *Recognition and prevention of major mental and substance use disorders* (pp. 1-20). Washington, DC: American Psychiatric Press.

Gonzalez-Gordon, R. G., Salvador-Carulla, L., Romero, C., Gonzalez-Saiz, F., & Romero, D. (2002). Feasibility, reliability, and validity of the Spanish version of Psychiatric Assessment Schedule for Adults with Developmental Disability: A structured psychiatric interview for intellectual disability. *Journal of Intellectual Disability Research, 46,* 209-217.

Gothelf, D., Feinstein, C., Thompson, T., Gu, E., Penniman, L., Van Stone, E., et al. (2007). Risk factors for the emergence of psychotic disorders in adolescents with 22q11.2 deletion syndrome. *American Journal of Psychiatry, 164,* 663-669.

Greenspan, S. I. & Wieder, S. (2007). *Infant and early childhood mental health: A comprehensive developmental approach to assessment and intervention.* Washington, DC: American Psychiatric Publishing, Inc.

Gregory, A. M., Caspi, A., Moffitt, T. E., Koenen, K., Elev, T. C., & Poulton, R. (2007). Juvenile mental health histories of adults with anxiety disorders. *American Journal of Psychiatry, 164,* 301-308.

Grinker, R. R. (2007). *Unstrange minds: Remapping the world of autism.* New York: Basic Books.

Gustafsson, C. & Sonnander, K. (2002). Psychometric evaluation of a Swedish version of the Reiss Screen for Maladaptive Behavior. *Journal of Intellectual Disability Research, 46,* 218-229.

Helsel, W. J., & Matson, J. L. (1988). The relationship of depression to social skills and intellectual functioning in mentally retarded adults. *Journal of Mental Deficiency Research, 32,* 411-418.

Hendrin, R. L. & Mullen, D. J. (2006). Conduct disorder and oppositional defiant disorder. In M. K. Dulcan & J. M. Wiener (Eds.), *Essentials of child and adolescent psychiatry* (pp. 357-385). Washington, DC: American Psychiatric Publishing, Inc.

Henry, J., Sloane, M., & Black-Pond, C. (2007). Neurobiology and neurodevelopmental impact of childhood traumatic stress and prenatal alcohol exposure. *Language, Speech, & Hearing Services in Schools, 38,* 99-108.

Hoekstra, P. J. & Minderaa, R. B. (2005). Tic disorders and obsessive-compulsive disorder: Is autoimmunity involved?. *International Review of Psychiatry, 17,* 497-502.

Holtmann, M., Bolte, S., & Poustka, F. (2007). Autism spectrum disorders: Sex difference in autistic behaviour domains and coexisting psychopathology. *Developmental Medicine & Child Neurology, 49,* 361-366.

Homaki, E., Rasanen, P. Viilo, K., Hakko, H: STUDY-70 Workgroup (2007). Suicidal behavior among adolescents with conduct disorder: The role of alcohol dependence. *Psychiatry Research, 150,* 305-311.

Hotz, R. L. (2007, July 6). Study of kids' brains hopes to answer: What is normal?. *Wall Street Journal,* p. B1.

Hounie, A. G., Pauls, D. L., do Rosario-Campos, M. C., Mercadante, M. T., Diniz, J. B., De Mathis, M. A. et al. (2007). Obsessive-compulsive spectrum disorders and rheumatic fever: A family study. *Biologic Psychiatry, 61,* 266-272.

Hotz, R. L. (2008, March 21). Tiny gene variations can even alter effect of the pills we take. *Wall Street Journal*, p.B1.

Hudziak, J. J. (Ed.) (2008). *Developmental psychopathology and wellness: Genetic and environmental influences.* Washington, DC: American Psychiatric Press, Inc.

Hurley, A. D. (1996, Jan./Feb./Mar). Identifying psychiatric disorders in persons with mental retardation: A model illustrated by depression in Down syndrome. *Journal of Rehabilitation*, 27-33.

Hurley, A. D. (1998). Two cases of suicide attempt by patients with Down's syndrome. *Psychiatric Services, 49*, 1618-1619.

Jan, J. I., Abroms, I. F., Freeman, R. D., Brown, G. M., Espezel, H., & Connolly, M. B. (1994). Rapid cycling in severely multi-disabled children: A form of bipolar affective disorder?. *Pediatric Neurology, 10*, 34-39.

Jaycox, L. H., Tanielian, T. L., Sharma, B. A., Morse, L., Clum, G., & Stein, B. D. (2007). Schools' mental health responses after hurricanes Katrina and Rita. *Psychiatric Services, 58*, 1339-1343.

Jellink, M., Patel, B. P., & Froehle, M. C. (Eds.). (2002a). *Bright futures in practice: Mental health (Vol. I).* Arlington, VA: National Center for Education in Maternal & Child Health.

Jellink, M., Patel, B. P., & Froehle, M. C. (Eds.). (2002b). *Bright futures in practice: Mental health (Vol. II).* Arlington, VA: National Center for Education in Maternal & Child Health.

Jenkins, R., Rose, J., & Jones, T. (1998). The Checklist of Challenging Behaviour and its relationship with the Psychopathology Inventory for Mentally Retarded Adults. *Journal of Intellectual Disability Research, 42*, 273-278.

John, P. B., Russell, S., & Russell, P. S. (2007). The prevalence of posttraumatic stress disorder among children and adolescents affected by tsunami disaster in Tamil Nadu. *Disaster Management Response, 5*, 3-7.

Jolin, E. M., Weller, E. B., & Weller, R. A. (2007). The public health aspects of bipolar disorder in children and adolescents. *Current Psychiatry Reports, 9*, 106-113.

Kaplow, J. B. & Widom, C. S. (2007). Age of onset of child maltreatment predicts long-term mental health outcomes. *Journal of Abnormal Psychology, 116,* 176-187.

Kazdin, A. E., Matson, J. L., & Senatore, V. (1983). Assessment of depression in mentally retarded adults. *American Journal of Psychiatry, 140,* 1040-1043.

Kenardy, J. A., Spence, S. H., & Macleod, A. C. (2006). Screening for posttraumatic stress disorder in children after accidental injury. *Pediatrics, 118,* 1002-1009.

Kim-Cohen, J., Caspi, A., Rutter, M., Tomas, M. P., & Moffitt, T. E. (2006). The caregiving environments provided to children by depressed mothers with or without an antisocial history. *American Journal of Psychiatry, 163,* 1009-1018.

Kirn, T. F. (2003, Feb. 15). Right temporal abnormality: Epilepsy and depression may share biologic link. *Family Practice News,* p. 16.

Koenen, K. C., Moffitt, T. E., Poulton, R., Martin, J., & Caspi, A. (2007). Early childhood factors associated with the development of post-traumatic stress disorder: Results from a longitudinal birth cohort. *Psychological Medicine, 37,* 181-192.

Kroll, L., Rothwell, J., Bradley, D., Shah, P., Bailey, S., & Harrington, R. C. (2002). Mental health needs of boys in secure care for serious or persistent offending: A prospective, longitudinal study. *Lancet, 359,* 1975-1979.

Kumra, S., Nicholson, R., & Rapoport, J. L. (2002). Childhood-onset schizophrenia: Research update. In R. B. Zipursky & S. C. Schulz (Eds.), *The early stages of schizophrenia* (pp. 161-190). Washington, DC: American Psychiatric Publishing, Inc.

Laman, D. S., & Reiss, S. (1987). Social skill deficiencies associated with depressed mood of mentally retarded adults. *American Journal on Mental Deficiency, 92,* 224-229.

Lee, P. & Friedlander, R. (2007). Attention-deficit and disruptive behavior disorders. In R. Fletcher, E. Loschen, C. Stavrakaki, & M. First (Eds.), *Diagnostic manual—intellectual disability* (pp. 127-144). Kingston, NY: NADD Press.

Lesse, S. (1979). Behavioral problems masking depression—cultural and clinical survey. *American Journal of Psychotherapy, 33*, 41-53.

Leverich, G. S., Post, R. M., Keck, P. E. Jr., Altshuler, L. L., Frye, M. A., Kupka, R. W., et al. (2007). The poor prognosis of childhood-onset bipolar disorder. *Journal of Pediatrics, 150*, 485-490.

Lindsay, W. R., Michie, A. M., Baty, F. J., Smith, A. H., & Miller, S. (1994). The consistency of reports about feelings and emotions from people with intellectual disability. *Journal of Intellectual Disability Research, 38*, 61-66.

Liu, X., Hubbard, J. A., Fabes, R. A., & Adam, J. B. (2006). Sleep disturbances and correlates of children with autism spectrum disorders. *Child Psychiatry & Human Development, 37*, 179-191.

Lofthouse, N., Fristad, M., Splaingard, M., & Kelleber, K. (2007). Parent and child reports of sleep problems associated with early-onset bipolar spectrum disorders. *Journal of Family Psychology, 21*, 114-123.

Lowry, M. A. (1998). Assessment and treatment of mood disorders in persons with developmental disabilities. *Journal of Developmental & Physical Disabilities, 10*, 387-406.

Luby, J. & Belden, A. (2006). Defining and validating bipolar disorder in the preschool period. *Developmental Psychopathology, 18*, 971-988.

Luby, J., Tandon, M., & Nicol, G. (2007). Three clinical cases of DSM-IV mania symptoms in preschoolers. *Journal of Child & Adolescent Psychopharmacology, 17*, 237-243.

Mandell, D. S., Ittenbach, R. F., Levy, S. E., & Pinto-Martin, J. A. (2007). Disparities in diagnoses received prior to a diagnosis of autism spectrum disorder. *Journal of Autism & Developmental Disorders, 37*, 1795-1802.

Manikam, R., Matson, J. L., Coe, D. A., & Hillman, N. (1995). Adolescent depression: Relationships of self-report to intellectual and adaptive functioning. *Research in Developmental Disabilities, 16*, 349-364.

March, D. & Susser, E. (2008). Social context and developmental psychopathology. In J. J. Hudziak (Ed.), *Developmental psychopathology and wellness: Genetic and environmental influences* (pp. 49-64). Washington, DC: American Psychiatric Press, Inc.

Marteinsdottir, I., Svensson, A., Svedberg, M., Anderberg, U. M., & von Knorring, L. (2007). The role of life events in social phobia. *Nordic Journal of Psychiatry, 61,* 207-212.

Masi, G. (1998). Psychiatric illness in mentally retarded adolescents: Clinical features. *Adolescence, 33,* 425-434.

Masi, G., Brovedani, P., Mucci, M., & Favilla, L. (2002). Assessment of anxiety and depression in adolescents with mental retardation. *Child Psychiatry & Human Development, 32,* 227-237.

Masi, G. Perugi, G., Millepiedi, S. M., Mucci, M., Toni, C., Bertini, N., et al. (2006). Developmental differences according to age at onset in juvenile bipolar disorder. *Journal of Child & Adolescent Psychopharmacology, 16,* 679-685.

Matson, J. L., Barrett, R. P., & Helsel, W. J. (1988). Depression in mentally retarded children. *Research in Developmental Disabilities, 9,* 39-46.

Matson, J. L., Kazdin, A. E., & Senatore, V. (1984). Psychometric properties of the Psychopathology Instrument for Mentally Retarded Adults. *Applied Research in Mental Retardation, 5,* 81-89.

Matson, J. L. & Nebel-Schwalm, M. A. (2006, June 7, Epub ahead of print). Comorbid psychopathology with autism spectrum disorder in children: An overview. *Research in Developmental Disabilities.*

McBrien, J. A. (2003). Assessment and diagnosis of depression in people with intellectual disability. *Journal of Intellectual Disability Research, 47,* 1-13.

McDougle, C. J., Kresch, L. E., Goodman, W. K., Naylor, S. T., Volkmar, F. R., Cohen, D. J. et al. (1995). A case-controlled study of repetitive thoughts and behavior in adults with autistic disorder and obsessive-compulsive disorder. *American Journal of Psychiatry, 152,* 772-777.

McConachie, H., Randle, V., Hammal, D., & LeCouteur, A. (2005). A controlled trial of a training course for parents of children with suspected autism spectrum disorder. *Journal of Pediatrics, 147*, 283-284.

McDermott, S., Platt, T., & Krishnaswami, S. (1997). Are individuals with mental retardation at high risk for chronic disease?. *Family Medicine, 29*, 429-434.

McGlynn, T. J. & Metcalf, H. L. (Eds.) (1989). *Diagnosis and treatment of anxiety disorders: A physician's handbook.* Washington, DC: American Psychiatric Press.

Meiser-Stedman, R., Smith, P., Glucksman, E., Yule, W., & Dalgleish, T. (2007). Parent and child agreement for acute stress disorder, post-traumatic stress disorder and other psychopathology in a prospective study of children and adolescents exposed to single-event trauma. *Journal of Abnormal Child Psychology, 35*, 191-201.

Meshane, G., Bazzano, C., Walter, G., & Barton, G. (2007). Outcome of patients attending a specialist educational and mental health service for social anxiety disorders. *Clinical Child Psychology & Psychiatry, 12*, 117-124.

Meyers, B. A. (1998). Major depression in persons with moderate to profound mental retardation: Clinical presentation and case illustrations. *Mental Health Aspects of Developmental Disabilities, 1*, 57-68.

Monuteaux, M. C., Blacker, D., Beiderman, J., Fitzmarice, G., & Buka, S. L. (2006). Maternal smoking during pregnancy and offspring overt and covert conduct problems: A longitudinal study. *Journal of Child Psychology & Psychiatry, 47*, 883-890.

Morihisa, J. M., Cross, C. D., Price, S., Precioso, M., & Koontz, S. (2003). Laboratory and other diagnostic tests in psychiatry. In R. E. Hales & S. C. Yudofsky (Eds.), *Textbook of clinical psychiatry* (4th ed.), pp. 219-256. Washington, DC: American Psychiatric Publishing, Inc.

Moss, S., Prosser, H., Ibbotson, B., & Goldberg, D. (1996). Respondent and informant accounts of psychiatric symptoms in a sample of patients with learning disability. *Journal of Intellectual Disability Research, 40*, 457-465.

Mudford, O. C., Barrera, F. J., Murray, A., Boundy, K., Caldwell, K., & Goldberg, B. (1995). The dexamethasone suppression test and the diagnosis of depression in adults with severe and profound developmental disabilities. *Journal of Intellectual Disability Research, 39,* 275-283.

Naidu, A., James, I., Mukatoeva-Ladinska, E., & Briel, R. (2006, March 9). Diagnosis of Asperger syndrome in a 66-year-old male presenting with depression. *International Psychogeriatrica,* 1-3.

National Institute of Neurological Disorders & Stroke. (2005). *Emotional and Behavioral Health in Persons with Mental Retardation/Developmental Disabilities: Research Challenges and Opportunities* (Workshop summary, November 29 – December 1, 2001). Retrieved January 8, 2008 from www.ninds.nih. gov/news_and_events/proceedings/Emotional_Behavioral_ Health_2001.htm

Newman, C. L. & Motta, R. W. (2007). The effects of aerobic exercise on childhood PTSD, anxiety, and depression. *International Journal of Emergency Mental Health, 9,* 133-158.

Nilsen, W. (2007). Fostering futures: a preventive intervention program for school-age children in foster care. *Clinical Child Psychology & Psychiatry, 12,* 45-63.

Nylander, L., & Gillberg, C. (2001). Screening for autism spectrum disorders in adult psychiatric out-patients: A preliminary report. *Acta Psychiatrica Scandinavica, 103,* 428-434.

Patel, P., Goldberg, D., & Moss, S. (1993). Psychiatric morbidity in older people with moderate and severe learning disability. II: The prevalence study. *British Journal of Psychiatry, 163,* 481-491.

Pat-Horenczyk, R., Abramovitz, R., Peled, O., Brom, D., Daie, A., & Chemtob, C. M. (2007). Adolescent exposure to recurrent terrorism in Insrael: Posttraumatic distress and functional impairment. *American Journal of Orthopsychiatry, 77,* 76-85.

Patja, K., Livanainen, M., Raitasuo, S., & Lonnqvist, J. (2001). Suicide mortality in mental retardation: A 35-year follow-up study. *Acta Psychiatrica Scandinavica, 103,* 307-311.

Paul, L. A., Gray, M. J., Elhai, J. D., Massad, P. M., & Stamm, B. H. (2006). Promotion of evidence-based practices for child traumatic stress in rural populations: Identification of barriers and promising solutions. *Trauma, Violence, & Abuse, 7,* 260-273.

Pennington, B. F. (2002). *The development of psychopathology: Nature and nurture.* New York: Guilford Press.

Poindexter, A. R. (2002). *Assessment and management of sleep disorders in persons with developmental disabilities.* Kingston, NY: NADD Press.

Popper, C. W., Gammon, G. D., West, S. A., & Bailey, C. E. (2003). Disorders usually first diagnosed in infancy, childhood, or adolescence. In R. E Hales & S. C. Yudofsky (Eds.), *Textbook of clinical psychiatry* (4th ed.), pp. 833-974. Washington, DC: American Psychiatric Publishing, Inc.

Powell, R. (2003). Psychometric properties of the Beck Depression Inventory and the Zung Self Rating Depression Scale in adults with mental retardation. *Mental Retardation, 41,* 88-95.

Prabhuswamy, M., Srinath, S., Girimaji, S., & Seshadri, S. (2007). Outcome of children with school refusal. *Indian Journal of Pediatrics, 74,* 375-379.

Prosser, H., Moss, S., Costello, H., Simpson, N., Patel, P., & Rowe, S. (1998). Reliability and validity of the Mini PASS-ADD for assessing psychiatric disorders in adults with intellectual disability. *Journal of Intellectual Disability Research, 42,* 264-272.

Prout, H. T., & Schaefer, B. M. (1985). Self-reports of depression by community-based mildly mentally retarded adults. *American Journal on Mental Deficiency, 90,* 220-222.

Reading, R. (2007). Parenting programme for parents of children at risk of developing conduct disorder: Cost effectiveness analysis. *Child Care & Health Development, 33,* 506-507.

Reiss, S. (1988). *The test manual for the Reiss Screen for maladaptive behavior.* Orland Park, IL: International Diagnostic Systems, Inc.

Reiss, S., & Rojahn, J. (1993). Joint occurrence of depression and aggression in children and adults with mental retardation. *Journal of Intellectual Disability Research, 37,* 287-294.

Reiss, S., & Szyskoo, J. (1983). Diagnostic overshadowing and professional experience with mentally retarded persons. *American Journal on Mental Deficiency, 87,* 396-402.

Reiss, S., & Valenti-Hein, D. (1990). *Reiss Scales for Children's Dual Diagnosis: Test manual.* Orland Park, IL: International Diagnostic Systems, Inc.

Rende, R., Birmaher, B., Axelson, D., Strober, M., Gill, M. K., Valeri, S., et al. (2007). Childhood-onset bipolar disorder: Evidence for increased familial loading of psychiatric illness. *Journal of the American Academy of Child & Adolescent Psychiatry, 46,* 197-204.

Reynolds, W. M., & Baker, J. A. (1988). Assessment of depression in persons with mental retardation. *American Journal on Mental Retardation, 93,* 93-103.

Reiersen, A. M., Neuman, R. J., Reich, W., Constantino, J. N., Volk, H. E., & Todd, R. D. (2008). Intersection of autism and ADHD. In Hudziak, J. J. (Ed.), *Developmental psychopathology and wellness: Genetic and environmental influences* (pp. 191-207). Washington, DC: American Psychiatric Press, Inc.

Rojahn, J., Warren, V. J., & Ohringer, S. (1994). A comparison of assessment methods for depression in mental retardation. *Journal of Autism and Developmental Disorders, 24,* 305-315.

Romansky, J. B., Lyons, J. S., Lehner, R. K., & West, C. M. (2003). Factors related to psychiatric hospital readmission among children and adolescents in state custody. *Psychiatric Services, 54,* 356-362.

Rowe, M. G., Fleming, M. F., Barry, K. L., Manwell, L. B., & Kropp, S. (1995). Correlates of depression in primary care. *The Journal of Family Practice, 41,* 551-558.

Rutter, M. (2008). Developing concepts in developing psychopathology. In J. J. Hudziak (Ed.), *Developmental psychopathology and wellness: Genetic and environmental influences* (pp. 3-22). Washington, DC: American Psychiatric Press, Inc.

Senatore, V., Matson, J. L., & Kazdin, A. E. (1985). An inventory to assess psychopathology of mentally retarded adults. *American Journal on Mental Deficiency, 89,* 459-466.

Sharp, L. K. & Lipsky, M. S. (2002). Screening for depression across the lifespan: A review of measures for use in primary care settings. *American Family Physician, 66,* 1001-1008.

Smoller, J. W. & Korf, B. R. (2008). The road ahead. In J. W. Smoller, B. R. Sheidley, & M. T. Tsuang (Eds.), *Psychiatric genetics: Applications in clinical practice* (pp. 277-309). Washington, DC: American Psychiatric Press, Inc.

Smoller, J. W., Sheidley, B. R., & Tsuang, M. T. (Eds.) (2008). *Psychiatric genetics: Applications in clinical practice.* Washington, DC: American Psychiatric Press, Inc.

Solomon, M., Hessl, D., Chiu, S., Hagerman, R., & Hendren, R. (2007). A genetic etiology of pervasive developmental disorder guides treatment. *American Journal of Psychiatry, 164,* 575-580.

Sourander, A., Haavisto, A. Ronning, J. A., Multimaki, P., Parkkola, K., Santalahti, P., et al. (2005). Recognition of psychiatric disorders, and self-perceived problems: A follow-up study from age 8 to age 18. *Journal of Child Psychology & Psychiatry, 46,* 1124-1134.

Sovner, R. (1990, December). *Differential diagnosis of violence.* Paper presented at the meeting of the National Association for the Dually Diagnosed, Boston, MA.

Sovner, R., & Fogelman, S. (1996). Irritability and mental retardation. *Seminars in Clinical Neuropsychiatry, 1,* 105-114.

Sovner, R., & Hurley, A. D. (1983). Do the mentally retarded suffer from affective illness?. *Archives of General Psychiatry, 40,* 61-67.

Sovner, R., & Hurley, A. D. (1989). Ten diagnostic principles for recognizing psychiatric disorders in mentally retarded persons. *Psychiatric Aspects of Mental Retardation Reviews, 8,* 9-13.

Sovner, R., Hurley, A. D., & LaBrie, R. A. (1982). Diagnosing depression in the mentally retarded. *Psychiatric Aspects of Mental Retardation Newsletter, 1,* 1-4.

Stein, M. B. (2006). An epidemiologic perspective on social anxiety disorder. *Journal of Clinical Psychiatry, 67 (suppl. 12)*, 3-8.

Stewart, M. E., Barnard, L., Pearson, J., Hasan, R., & O'Brien, G. (2006). Presentation of depression in autism and Asperger syndrome: A review. *Autism, 10*, 103-116.

Stewart, S. E., Ceranoglu, T. A., O'Hanley, T., & Geller, D. A. (2005). Performance of clinician versus self-report measures to identify obsessive-compulsive disorder in children and adolescents. *Journal of Child & Adolescent Psychopharmacology, 15*, 956-963.

Sturmey, P., Reed, J., & Corbett, J. (1991). Psychometric assessment of psychiatric disorders in people with learning difficulties (mental handicap): A review of measures. *Psychological Medicine, 21*, 143-155.

Tarrart, L., McLaughlin, D., Quinn, B., & Milligan, V. (2006). An exploration of substance misuse in people with intellectual disabilities. *Journal of Intellectual Disability Research, 50*, 588-597.

Tsai, L. Y. (2006). Autistic disorders. In M. K. Dulcan & J. M. Wiener (Eds.), *Essentials of child and adolescent psychiatry* (pp. 153-201). Arlington, VA: American Psychiatric Publishing, Inc.

Tsai, L. Y. & Champine, D. J. (2006). Schizophrenia and other psychotic disorders. In M. K. Dulcan & J. M. Wiener (Eds.), *Essentials of child and adolescent psychiatry* (pp. 235-263). Arlington, VA: American Psychiatric Publishing, Inc.

Tsakanikos, E., Costello, H., Holt, G., Bouras, N., Sturmey, P., & Newton. T. (2006). Psychopathology in adults with autism and intellectual disability. *Journal of Autism & Developmental Disorders, 36*, 1123-1129.

Volkmar, F. R., & Cohen, D. J. (1991). Comorbid association of autism and schizophrenia. *American Journal of Psychiatry, 148*, 1705-1707.

Vollner, S. (2002). Depression: Meeting the clinical challenge. *Family Practice Recertification, 24 (9)*, 25-40.

Vorstman, J. A., Morcus, M. E., Duijff, S. N., Klaassen, P. W., Heineman-de Boer, J. A., Swab, H., et al. (2006). The 22q11.2 deletion in children: High rate of autistic disorders and early onset of psychotic symptoms. *Journal of the American Academy of Child & Adolescent Psychiatry, 45*, 1104-1113.

Wamboldt, M. Z. & Reiss, D. (2006). Editorial: Explorations of parenting environments in the evolution of psychiatric problems in children. *American Journal of Psychiatry, 163*, 951-953.

Wang, Y., Nomura, Y., Pat-Horenczyk, R., Doppelt, O., Abramovitz, R. Brom, D., & Chemtob, C. (2006). Association of direct exposure to terrorism, medica exposure to terrorism, and other trauma with emotional and behavioral problems in preschool children. *Annals of the N.Y. Academy of Science, 1094*, 363-368.

Waslick, B. & Greenhill, L. L. (2006). Attention-deficit/hyperactivity disorder. In M. K. Dulcan & J. M. Wiener (Eds.), *Essentials of child and adolescent psychiatry* (pp. 323-354). Arlington, VA: American Psychiatric Publishing Co.

Witt, W. P., Kasper, J. D., & Riley, A. W. (2003). Mental health services use among school-aged children with disabilities: The role of sociodemographics, functional limitations, family burdens, and care coordination. *Health Services Research, 38*, 1441-1466.

Yamasue, H., Ishijima, M., Abe, O., Sasaki, T., Yamada, H., Suga, M., et al. (2005). Neuroanatomy in monozygotic twins with Asperger disorder discordant for comorbid depression. *Neurology, 65*, 491-492.

Youth suicides on the rise—question is why? (2007, Oct. 5). *Psychiatric News, 42(19)*, 4.

Zung, W. W. K., Broadhead, W. E., & Roth, M. E. (1993). Prevalence of depressive symptoms in primary care. *The Journal of Family Practice, 37*, 337-344.

SUGGESTED HELPFUL WEB SITES

International Foundation for Research and Education on Depression (iFred): www.ifred.org

Mental Health America (formerly National Mental Health Association): www.mentalhealthamerica.net

National Depressive and Manic Depressive Association Depression and Bipolar Support Alliance (DBSA): www.ndmda.org

National Institute of Neurological Disorders & Stroke:

www.ninds.nih.gov/news_and_events/proceedings/Emotional_Behavioral_Health_2001.htm

National Library of Medicine: http://medlineplus.gov

INDEX

A

E

F

G

H

Hallucinations 61
Hamilton Rating Scale for Depression 22
Health, Effect on 1
Hurricanes 47

I

ID 8, 9, 10, 11, 12, 13, 14, 15, 16, 18, 19, 20, 21, 22, 23, 24, 25, 26,
    27, 29, 31, 35, 39, 49, 50, 53, 58, 61, 67, 68, 74, 80
  and ADHD 58
  and Autism Spectrum Disorders 68
Inattention and Hyperactivity 57
Increased Arousal 44
Increased Vulnerability 6
Increased Vulnerability to Acccidents 58
Inflated Self-Esteem 32
Intellectual Disability Issues
  Conduct Disorder 53-54
  Depression 18-21

M

Manic Episode
  Criteria for 31
Marston 30 Symptoms Checklist 27
Maternal Depression 17
Mini PASS-ADD 24
Modified Criteria
  Depression 20

N

Nature and Nurture 17, 40

O

Obsessive-Compulsive Disorder *See* OCD
OCD 49-51, 69
  and Autism 69
  Childhood and Adolescent Issues 51
  Diagnostic Criteria 49-50
  Diagnostic Considerations 50
ODD
  and Bipolar Disorder 34

P

Panic Attack 37
Parent's Guide to Building Resilience in Children and Teens: Giving Your Child Roots and Wings 5, 72
PASS-ADD 10, 24
PDD 17
Pervasive Developmental Disorders. *See* PDD
PIMRA 22, 25, 26
Positive Social Supports 28
Post-traumatic Stress Disorder. *See* PTSD
Predictability of Future Disorders 2
Prenatal Alcohol 3
Pressured Speech and Racing Thoughts 32
Prevalence 1
  Anxiety 37
  Autism Spectrum Disorders 65
  Bipolar Disorder 31
  Depression 7-8
Prevalence in Persons with ID
  Depression 8-10
Prevention and Amelioration
  Anxiety 41
  Autism Spectrum Disorders 71-72
  Bipolar Disorder 33

Y

Z